BASIC ASTROLOGY
A WORK BOOK FOR STUDENTS

JOAN NEGUS

Published by
ACS Publications, Inc.
P.O Box 16430
San Diego, California 92116

International Standard Book Number 0-917086-15-5

Published by ACS Publications, Inc.
P.O. Box 34487
San Diego, CA 92163

Printed in the United States of America

First printing, June 1978
Second printing, December 1982
Third printing, March 1987
Fourth printing, August 1990

CONTENTS

PREFACE

This workbook consists of pages taken from my book *Basic Astrology: A Guide for Teachers and Students.* The workbook may be used in most beginning astrology courses with most basic texts since it covers all the usual introductory material. The order in which the principles are presented, however, varies from book to book and, therefore, using *Basic Astrology: A Guide for Teachers and Students* along with the workbook provides the most efficient way to utilize the materials. The text provides a succinct, cohesive method of teaching or learning astrology, and the workbook contains the parts that reinforce the memorization and understanding of the subject.

In teaching and developing the method over the last few years, I have noticed that the more systematic students keep corrected homework in a notebook for reference, whereas others have to leaf through materials to find pertinent information. The reference lists are particularly helpful for chart interpretation. The workbook places the material in a logical sequence and helps the student to avoid the temptation to "peek" at the answers, which are so easily accessible in the text.

Students seem to agree that the assignments are fun, give them a feeling of accomplishment and make the principles of astrology relatively simple to learn.

All of the essential homework sheets, charts and other materials from *Basic Astrology: A Guide for Teachers and Students* have been combined in this workbook. If each student has a copy of this Workbook the learning process is made easier because the assignments are ordered according to course sequence and the teacher is relieved of the chore of reproducing the materials. Students also grasp what is being taught in class more quickly when they have pertinent information to reinforce class lectures and for reference afterwards.

TEMPERAMENT PATTERNS
AND HEMISPHERE EMPHASIS

Hemisphere Emphasis

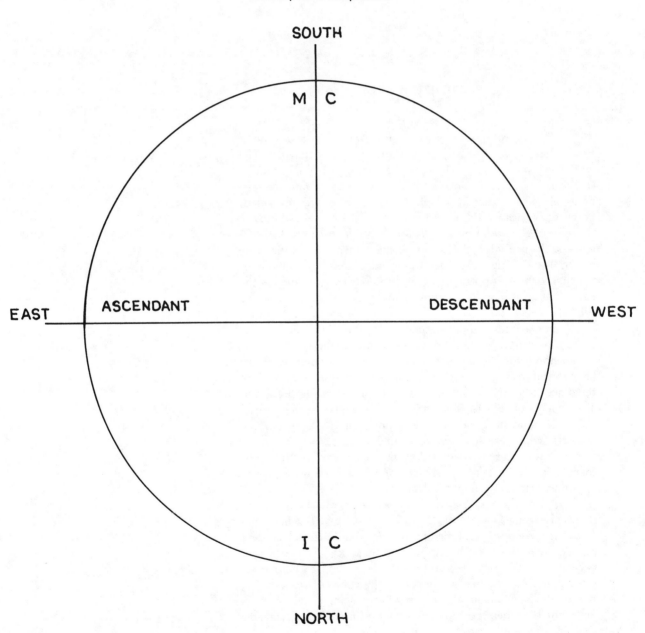

Splash: Theodore Roosevelt

Splash (an image of "scatteredness"). In the splash pattern the planets are in eight to ten different signs or houses. At best it indicates the universal man, interested in many things and knowing many of them well. At worst it is the jack-of-all-trades and master-of-none.

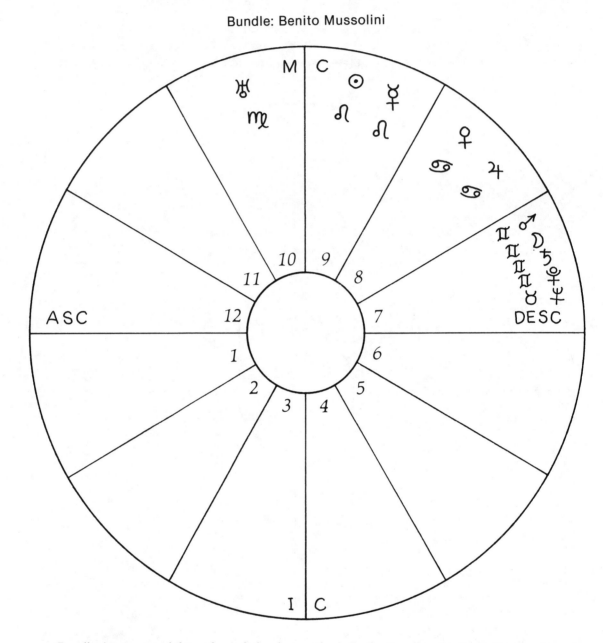

Bundle: Benito Mussolini

Bundle (an image of things bound closely together). In the Bundle pattern all the planets are within a trine (120º). This denotes an individual who has very narrow interests. Hemisphere emphasis individualizes the Bundle. A predominantly northeastern Bundle shows a person who is self-sufficient and adjusts the world to himself. A northwestern Bundle shows a person whose opportunities come from others, but then he adapts situations to himself.

A southeastern Bundle is indicative of an individual who initiates, but in terms of adjusting to the world. A southwestern Bundle is reflective of a person who adjusts to the world, trying to do what is expected of him. His opportunities come from others. It is possible that the Bundle will not be entirely within one quadrant, and, therefore, the above definitions would have to be combined.

Locomotive: Henry Ford

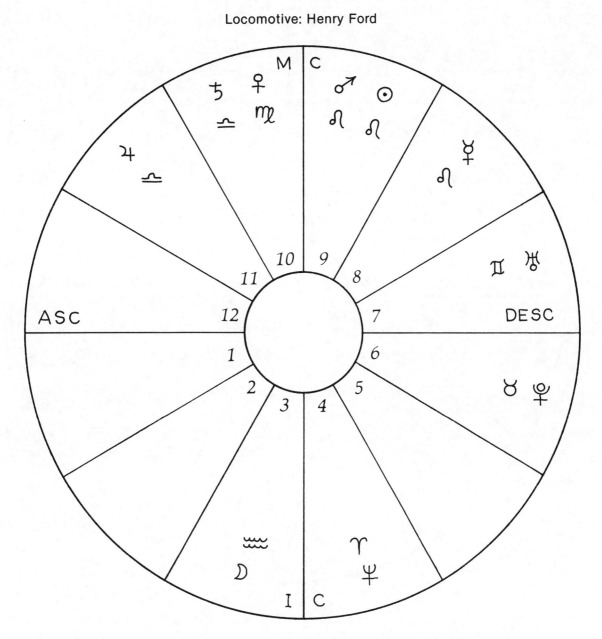

Locomotive (an image of hard-driving, forward action). In this pattern there is an empty trine (120°). All the planets are within 240°, with no more than a sextile (60°) from one to the next. An individual with a Locomotive pattern tends to be self-driving and dynamic. He can be a pioneer in some area.

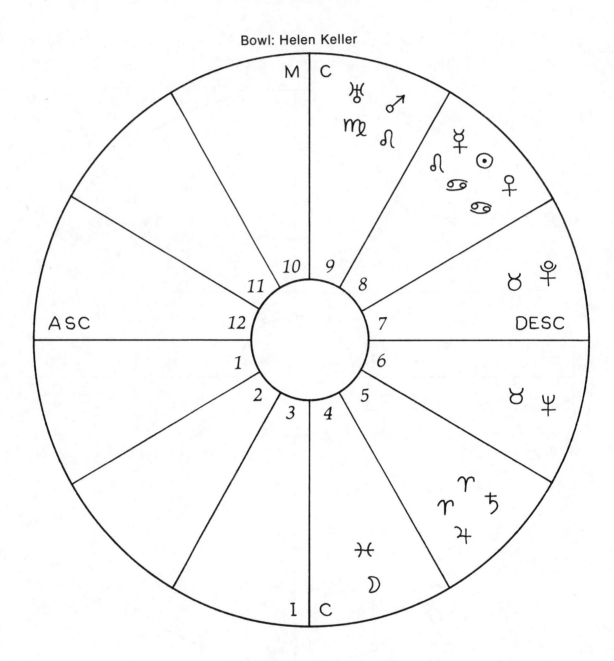

Bowl: Helen Keller

Bowl (the image of a container which holds liquid that is poured into it, the liquid taking on the shape of the container). In this configuration all of the planets are within one opposition (180°) and ideally are in six signs or houses. A person with a bowl pattern is self-contained and develops mainly through experience (as experience pours in, it takes on the shape of the individual). Hemisphere emphasis determines whether the individual keeps his development within himself (northern) or shares it with the world (southern); or if he initiates his experience (eastern), or if opportunities come from others for his experience (western). The Bowl will include at least two quadrants; therefore the hemisphere emphasis will be blended into the pattern interpretation.

Bucket: Marilyn Monroe

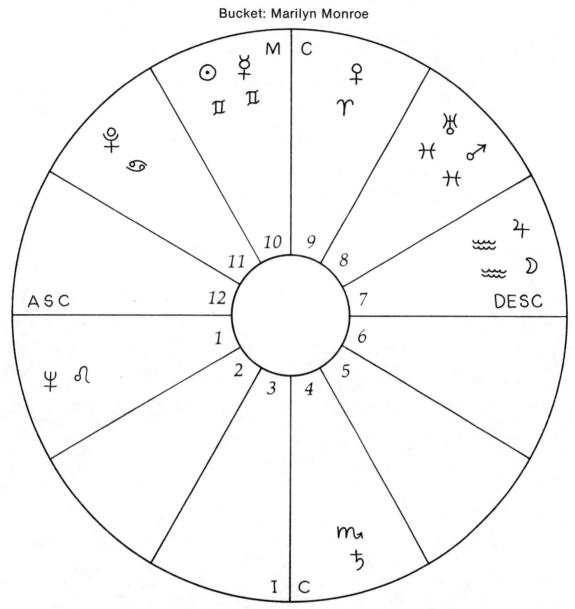

Bucket (the image of a container with a handle). In the Bucket pattern, ideally nine planets are in one half of the chart, within 180°, and one planet is in the other half of the chart opposing the nine. Or eight planets may be in one half of the chart, with two planets in conjunction opposing the eight. The eight or nine planets which are together form a "bowl," so that the definition of the Bucket also includes self-containment and development through experience. The one or two planets forming the "handle" add another element, however. This planet or these planets provide a point of release for the energy of the native. He must, in some way, give back to the world what he has experienced in the world, even if the native is primarily northern.

There is a variation of the Bucket wherein the eight or nine planets are within a trine (120°) resembling a Bundle rather than a Bowl. This variation signifies that this individual has narrower interests than the person with a Bowl. The handle still represents a point of release for the energy of the native. This pattern is called a "Bundle-Bucket."

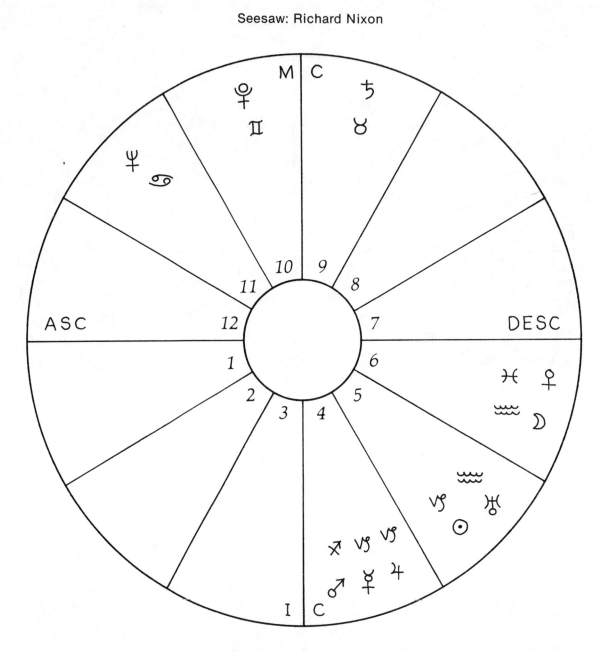

Seesaw: Richard Nixon

Seesaw (the image of a seesaw going up and down and connoting balance). In the seesaw pattern the planets fall in opposition to each other. Ideally, five planets oppose five others. It may be, however, that as many as seven planets will oppose three others. This configuration shows a need for the native to balance different areas and energies in his life, or the effect will be separative. What particularly must be balanced depends on the planets themselves, the signs and the houses involved.

Splay: Babe Ruth

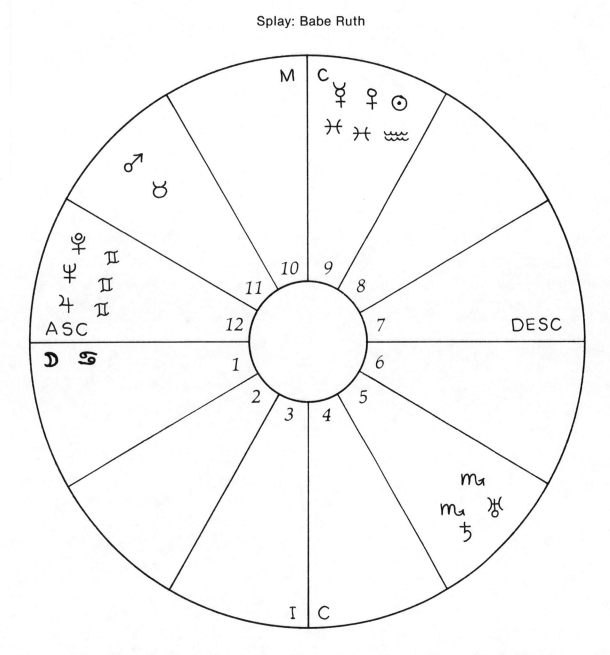

Splay (an image of a wheel with several spokes, not necessarily evenly spaced but holding the wheel together). In the Splay the planets fall into three, four or five groups, each usually involving a conjunction. Each spoke indicates an area of interest. A person with a splay configuration is usually an individualist. His interests will be few (generally as many as he has spokes), but these will be highly developed. He will delve deeply into whatever interests him.

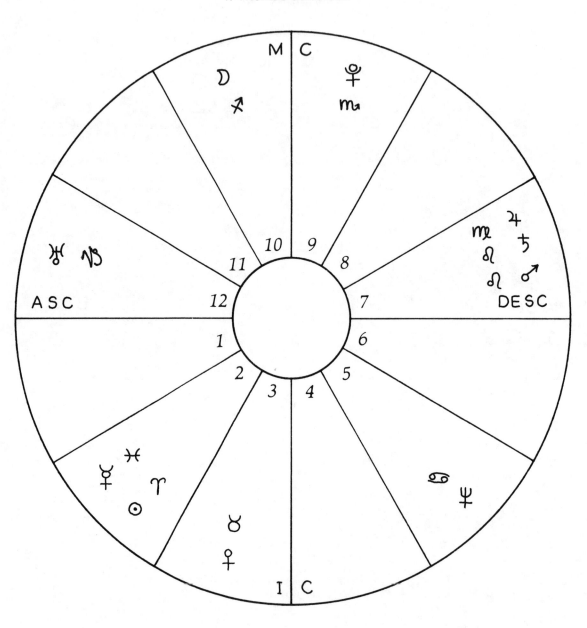

1: Thomas Jefferson

2: Edward Kennedy

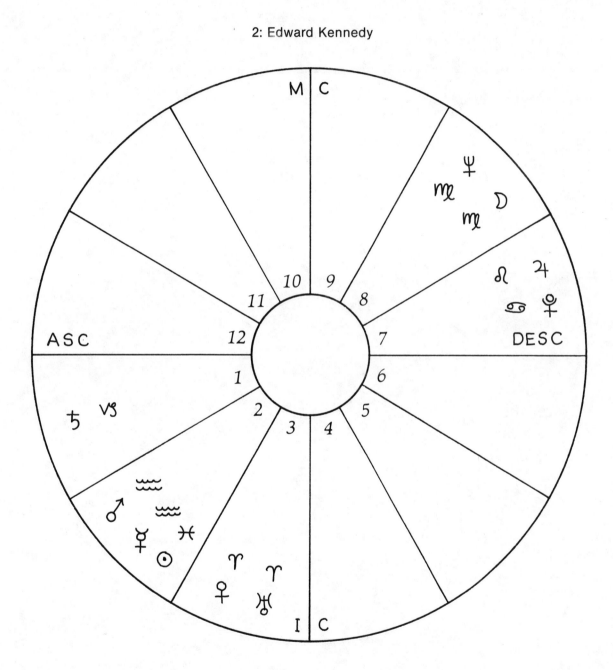

3: George Wallace

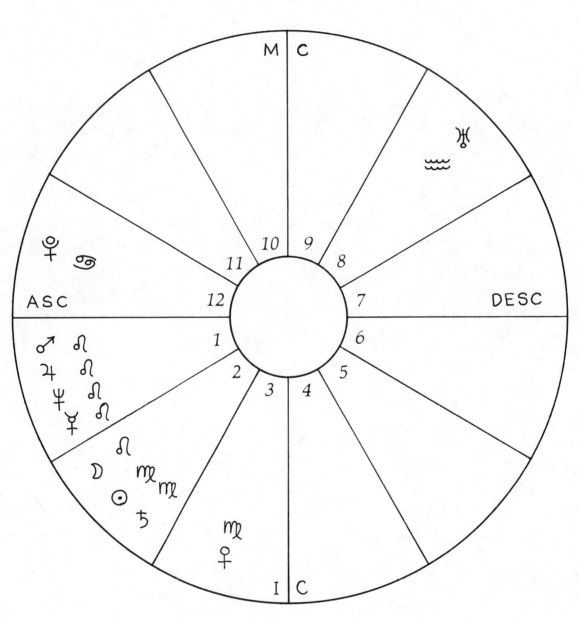

4: Eddie Rickenbacker

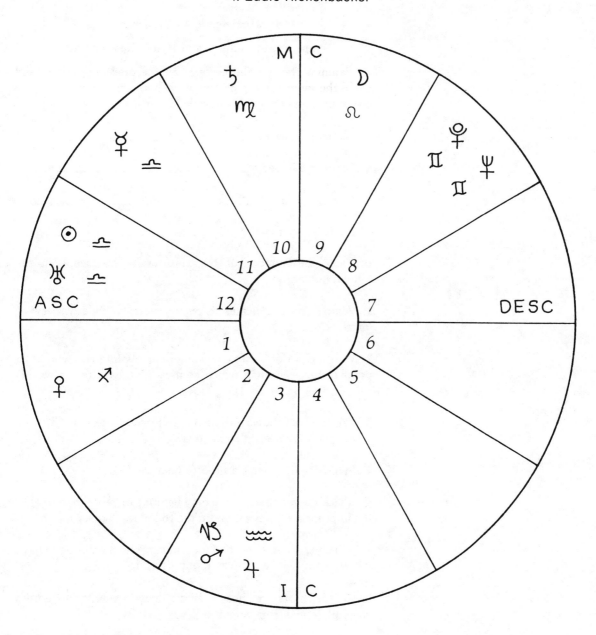

Homework Assignment

Temperament Patterns and Hemisphere Emphasis

A. Examine the four horoscopes on the preceding pages, and name the temperament pattern each horoscope has. (You may use your temperament pattern definitions).

1. Thomas Jefferson _____

2. Edward Kennedy _____

3. George Wallace _____

4. Eddie Rickenbacker _____

B. Place the number of the appropriate horoscope in the following blanks.

1. Which chart indicates a person with a wide variety of interests? _____

2. Which chart discloses a person of narrow interests who has a point of focus through which he must give back to the world? _____

3. Which chart shows a dynamic, self-driving person who may have been a pioneer in some area? _____

4. Which chart reveals a need to balance? _____

C. Place the numbers (there may be none or more than one) of the appropriate horoscopes in the following blanks.

1. Which charts are those of individuals who tend more to have initiative and make their own opportunities? _____

2. Which charts are those of individuals whose opportunities generally come from others? _____

3. Which charts are those of individuals who usually adjust to the world? _____

4. Which charts are those of individuals who usually adjust the world to them? _____

2

HOUSES AND PLANETS

Planet-Sign Rulerships

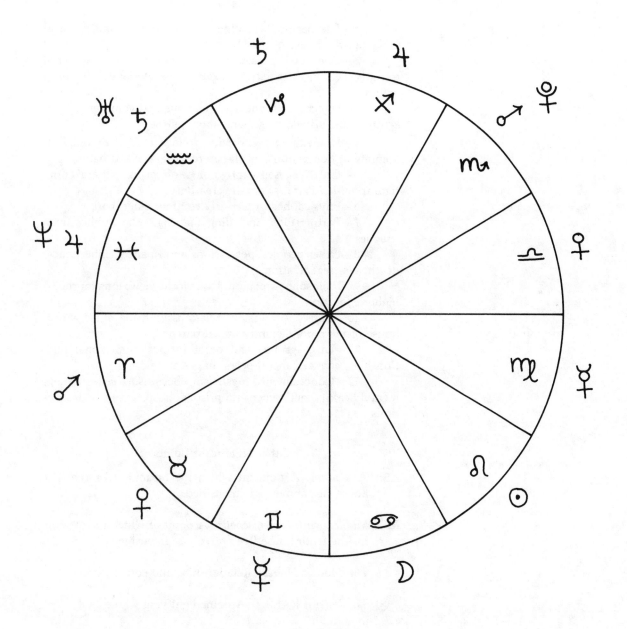

Basic Astrological Symbols and Concepts

Houses

1—The personality, physical appearance, and physical make-up; the house of the "I."

2—One's own possessions, finances, and other material resources; earning capacity, utilization of material objects, deep values.

3—Direct and immediate relations and communication, brothers and sisters, neighbors, short journeys.

4—Home, ancestry, origins, foundation, where one feels securely at home, house of the more closely-linked parent.

5—Creative self-expression; offspring, literal and figurative; love affairs, artistic creativity.

6—Physical health, service, routine, daily work.

7—Partnerships, including marriage; the public; open enemies.

8—Other peoples' possessions and finances, inheritance, death, sex, regeneration.

9—Philosophy, religion, law, world-view, long journeys, higher education.

10—Career, profession, relations with the outer world, house of the more distantly-linked parent.

11—Large groups and organizations, impersonal relationships, acquaintances, peers, hopes and wishes.

12—Concealment, mysticism, occultism, self-undoing, mental health, confinement (in prisons, hospitals, etc.), institutions.

Other Significant Points

ASC *Ascendant:* A point at which the meanings for the first house (see above) are intensified.

MC *Midheaven (medium coeli):* A point at which the meanings for the tenth house (see above) are intensified.

☊☋ *The Moon's Nodes:* Relationships and connections.

⊗ *The Part of Fortune:* A point signifying wholeness, integration, unity of self.

Planets

⊙ *Sun:* Vitalization, the directly expressed self, exercise of ego-identity and will; the paternal function. Rules Leo.

☽ *Moon:* Response, emotion, intuition; the maternal function. Rules Cancer.

☿ *Mercury:* Verbal skills, communication, perception, logical thinking, cleverness, wit, which are functions of the "lower mind." Rules Gemini and Virgo.

♀ *Venus:* Love, affection, pleasure, artistry, harmonization; female sexuality. Rules Taurus and Libra.

♂ *Mars:* Initiative, aggressive action, courage, violence, passion; male sexuality. Rules Aries, co-rules Scorpio (with Pluto).

♃ *Jupiter:* Wide-ranging and complex thinking, wisdom, which are functions of the "higher mind;" joy, optimism, success, excess; expansion. Rules Sagittarius, co-rules Pisces (with Neptune).

♄ *Saturn:* Contraction, containment, crystallization, responsibility, structure, discipline, channeling, limitation, restriction,frustration, gloom, pessimism; punishment. Rules Capricorn and co-rules Aquarius (with Uranus).

♅ *Uranus:* Deviation, liberation, sudden or revolutionary change; technique and technology. Co-rules Aquarius (with Saturn).

♆ *Neptune:* Refined sensitivity, spirituality, dissolution, confusion, illusion, intoxication; ethereal and spiritual artistry. Co-rules Pisces (with Jupiter).

♇ *Pluto:* Total transformation through elimination and renewal, violence, subterranean (subconscious) eruption, unrelenting power; deep probing and analysis. Co-rules Scorpio (with Mars).

Signs

♈ *Aries:* Self-assertiveness, aggressiveness, zeal, naivete; the "eager-beaver" and "me-first" sign. Ruled by Mars.

♉ *Taurus:* Practicality, persistence, domination by habit, stubbornness, possessiveness; the "artsy-craftsy" sign. Ruled by Venus.

♊ *Gemini:* Adaptability, flexibility, fluctuation, gregariousness, articulateness, two-sidedness; the sociability sign. Ruled by Mercury.

♋ *Cancer:* Motherliness, protectiveness, self-protectiveness, sensitivity, moodiness, deep emotionality, intuitiveness; the "homebody" sign. Ruled by the Moon.

♌ *Leo:* Warm-heartedness, generosity, magnanimity, pomposity, dominating or domineering tendencies; the sign of the king or the actor. Ruled by the Sun.

♍ *Virgo:* Painstaking industriousness, devotedness to service, analytical and critical tendencies, interest in health and hygiene, hypochondria, detail-orientation; "fussbudget" of the Zodiac. Ruled by Mercury.

♎ *Libra:* Harmony, need for partnerships and marriage, artistic and aesthetic values, diplomacy and tact, indolence, indecisiveness; the balancing sign. Ruled by Venus.

♏ *Scorpio:* Emotional intensity, hard-driving and persistent aggressiveness, loyalty, pessimism; preoccupation with sex, death and regeneration; secretiveness; the sign of probing and penetrating. Co-ruled by Mars and Pluto.

♐ *Sagittarius:* Enthusiasm; urge to travel far and wide, both mentally and physically; interest in fun, athletics, the out-of-doors and animals; the sign of the "jovial philosopher." Ruled by Jupiter.

♑ *Capricorn:* Ambition, patience; tendencies to be conventional, conservative and traditional; status-orientation, discipline, strong sense of duty; the unrelenting climber of the Zodiac. Ruled by Saturn.

♒ *Aquarius:* Humanitarian idealism, impersonal detachment, urge to liberate or be liberated, nonconformity, egalitarianism; the liberal or revolutionary of the Zodiac. Co-ruled by Saturn and Uranus.

♓ *Pisces:* Compassion, empathy, self-sacrifice, intuitiveness, mysticism, spiritualism, nebulousness, vulnerability to delusion and/or victimization; the sign of suffering and/or salvation. Co-ruled by Jupiter and Neptune.

Aspects

♂ *Conjunction* (0°): Strong but mixed in quality, depending on the planets involved.

☍ *Opposition* (180°): Hard; a need to balance or may be separative; an aspect of relationship

△ *Trine* (120°): Soft; what flows easily.

☐ *Square* (90°): Hard; obstacles to be overcome; may be building blocks or stumbling blocks.

⁎ *Sextile* (60°): Soft; like the trine but less powerful; an aspect of help from others.

⊻ *Semi-sextile* (30°): Mixed and mild.

⚻ *Quincunx* (150°): Mixed and moderately strong; an aspect combining quite different or contradictory things, therefore, often quite difficult to evaluate.

Q *Quintile* (72°): Soft, subtle; involves creativity.

± *Bi-quintile* (144°): Same as quintile.

∠ *Semi-square* (45°): Same as square but less powerful.

⬚ *Sesqui-quadrate* (135°): Same as semi-square.

Major Configurations

T-Square: Two planets in opposition, and a third planet square to both—usually in the same mode (cardinal, fixed, mutable).

Grand Cross: Two planets in opposition and square two other planets in opposition—usually in the same mode.

Grand Trine: Three planets in trine to each other—usually in the same element (fire, earth, air, water).

Yod (or Finger of God): Two planets sextile each other, and both quincunx a third.

Cradle: Four planets in a series of sextiles.

Cradle with a Hood: Five planets in a series of sextiles.

Homework Assignment

Houses and Planets

A. The numbers in the left-hand column are the numbers of the houses. The words in columns two and three are definitions for the houses. Place the letters of the definitions next to the appropriate house number. There will be two answers for each.

1._____	a. open enemies	m. other people's money
2._____	b. physical health	n. the home
3._____	c. distant travel	o. the personality
4._____	d. marriage partners	p. career
5._____	e. organizations such as clubs	q. values
6._____	f. short journeys	r. creative self-expression
7._____	g. relations with the outer world	s. one's own earning capacity
8._____	h. philosophy	t. peer groups
9._____	i. physical appearance	u. communications
10._____	j. one's origins	v. children
11._____	k. daily work	w. death
12._____	l. mental health	x. institutions

B. In the first column are the planets. In columns two and three are two definitions for each planet. Place the letters of the appropriate definitions next to the appropriate planet.

☉ Sun _____	a. originality	k. elimination
☾ Moon _____	b. spiritualism	l. frustration
☿ Mercury _____	c. love	m. aggressiveness
♀ Venus _____	d. expansion	n. artistry
♂ Mars _____	e. responsibility	o. lower mind
♃ Jupiter _____	f. illusion	p. power
♄ Saturn _____	g. revolutionary activity	q. responsiveness
♅ Uranus _____	h. the will	r. initiative
♆ Neptune _____	i. optimism	s. cleverness
♇ Pluto _____	j. the maternal function	t. exercise of ego identity

C. Multiple choice. For one possible manifestation of the planet in the house, circle the appropriate answer.

1. Initiative in career
a. ♀ in 5th house   b. ♂ in 10th house   c. ♄ in 8th house

2. Wants power over partner
a. ☉ in 3rd house   b. ☿ in 9th house   c. ♇ in 7th house

3. Gets an advanced degree in philosophy
a. ♃ in 9th house   b. ♂ in 4th house   c. ☾ in 12th house

4. Responsibility in the home
a. ♄ in 4th house   b. ♆ in 6th house   c. ♅ in 2nd house

5. Moodiness
a. ☿ in 11th house   b. ☾ in 1st house   c. ♃ in 10th house

6. Communicates in a confused way
a. ♅ in 2nd house   b. ♄ in 7th house   c. ♆ in 3rd house

7. Originality with peer groups
a. ☉ in 12th house   b. ♅ in 11th house   c. ♇ in 2nd house

8. Ego involvement with children
a. ♆ in 9th house   b. ☿ in 6th house   c. ☉ in 5th house

9. Earning one's own living through cleverness
a. ☿ in 2nd house   b. ☉ in 11th house   c. ♅ in 4th house

10. Artistry as part of daily work
a. ♂ in 8th house   b. ♀ in 6th house   c. ♄ in 12th house

3

SIGNS

Sign	Glyph	Symbol	House Connection	Element	Mode	Polarity	Ruler	Parts of the Body	Key words
Aries	♈	Ram	1	Fire	**Cardinal**	+	♂	Head and Face	
Taurus	♉	Bull	2	Earth	Fixed	−	♀	Neck and Throat	
Gemini	♊	Twins	3	Air	Mutable	+	☿	Hands, Arms Lungs	
Cancer	♋	Crab	4	Water	Cardinal	−	☾	Stomach, Breast	
Leo	♌	Lion	5	Fire	Fixed	+	☉	Heart, Upper Spine	
Virgo	♍	Virgin	6	Earth	Mutable	−	☿	Intestines	
Libra	♎	Scales	7	Air	Cardinal	+	♀	Kidneys, Lower Spine	
Scorpio	♏	Scorpion	8	Water	Fixed	−	♂ ♀	Sex Organs, Bladder, Anus	
Sagittarius	♐	Archer	9	Fire	Mutable	+	♃	Thighs, Liver	
Capricorn	♑	Mountain Goat	10	Earth	Cardinal	−	♄	Knees	
Aquarius	♒	Water Bearer	11	Air	Fixed	+	♄ ♅	Calves and Ankles	
Pisces	♓	Fish	12	Water	Mutable	−	♃ ♆	Feet	

Homework Assignment

First Six Signs of the Zodiac

A. All other things being equal, which sign would make the better:

1. Secretary: Virgo ♍ , or Leo ♌
2. Playboy: Gemini ♊ , or Cancer ♋
3. Actor or Actress: Virgo ♍ , or Leo ♌
4. Governess: Aries ♈ , or Cancer ♋
5. Craftsman: Taurus ♉ , or Aries ♈
6. Salesman: Virgo ♍ , or Aries ♈

B. Emphasis of a sign (which may come from planets, Ascendant or MC being placed in the sign) will indicate certain characteristics. In which signs would the following characteristics most likely be manifested?

1. Stubbornness: Aries ♈ , or Taurus ♉
2. Sociability: Gemini ♊ , or Virgo ♍
3. Personal magnetism: Leo ♌ , or Cancer ♋
4. Meticulousness: Leo ♌ , or Virgo ♍
5. Initiative: Taurus ♉ , or Aries ♈
6. Motherliness: Gemini ♊ , or Cancer ♋

C.   Venus (♀) represents love. Indications of love can be found in various ways in different areas of the chart; but considering just Venus (♀) in the first six signs, which word would best describe how the individual would love?

1. Would ♀ in ♈ be aggressive or shy?
2. Would ♀ in ♉ be fickle or loyal?
3. Would ♀ in ♊ be fickle or loyal?
4. Would ♀ in ♋ be selfish or protective?
5. Would ♀ in ♌ be warm or dispassionate?
6. Would ♀ in ♍ be practical or impractical?

Last Six Signs of the Zodiac

A.   All other things being equal, which sign would make the better:

1. Occultist: Capricorn ♑ , or Pisces ♓
2. Revolutionary: Aquarius ♒ , or Pisces ♓
3. Surgeon: Scorpio ♏ , or Aquarius ♒
4. Artist: Sagittarius ♐ , or Libra ♎
5. President of a company: Capricorn ♑ , or Libra ♎
6. World traveler: Scorpio ♏ , or Sagittarius ♐

B.   Emphasis of a sign (which may come from planets, Ascendant or MC being placed in the sign) will indicate certain characteristics. In which signs would the following characteristics most likely be manifested?

1. Conservatism: Capricorn ♑ , or Aquarius ♒
2. Pessimism: Sagittarius ♐ , or Scorpio ♏
3. Empathy: Capricorn ♑ , or Pisces ♓
4. Joviality: Sagittarius ♐ , or Scorpio ♏
5. Balance: Libra ♎ , or Pisces ♓
6. Cause-orientation: Aquarius ♒ , or Libra ♎

C. Venus (♀) represents love. Indications of love can be found in various ways in different areas of the chart; but considering just Venus (♀) in the last six signs, which word would best describe how the individual would love?

1. Would ♀ in ♎ be erratic or balanced?
2. Would ♀ in ♏ be emotional or cool?
3. Would ♀ in ♐ be fickle or loyal?
4. Would ♀ in ♑ be demonstrative or reserved?
5. Would ♀ in ♒ be possessive or impersonal?
6. Would ♀ in ♓ be selfish or self-sacrificing?

The Signs of the Zodiac

A. Write the names of the signs of the Zodiac and draw the glyphs in numerical order (e.g., 1. Aries ♈ , etc.). Then circle the characteristic adjective which is appropriate for that sign.

1. _____ is outgoing, passive.
2. _____ is stubborn, flexible.
3. _____ is unfriendly, sociable.
4. _____ is home-loving, career-oriented.
5. _____ is cold, warm.
6. _____ is sloppy, meticulous.
7. _____ is balanced, flighty.
8. _____ is shallow, intense.
9. _____ is morose, jovial.
10. _____ is conservative, radical.
11. _____ is passionate, interested in humanitarian causes.
12. _____ is sensitive, insensitive.

B. Triplicities:

1. Name the three fire signs._____
2. Name the three earth signs._____
3. Name the three air signs._____
4. Name the three water signs._____

C. Quadruplicities:

1. Name the four cardinal signs._____
2. Name the four fixed signs._____
3. Name the four mutable signs._____

4

ASPECTS AND MAJOR CONFIGURATIONS

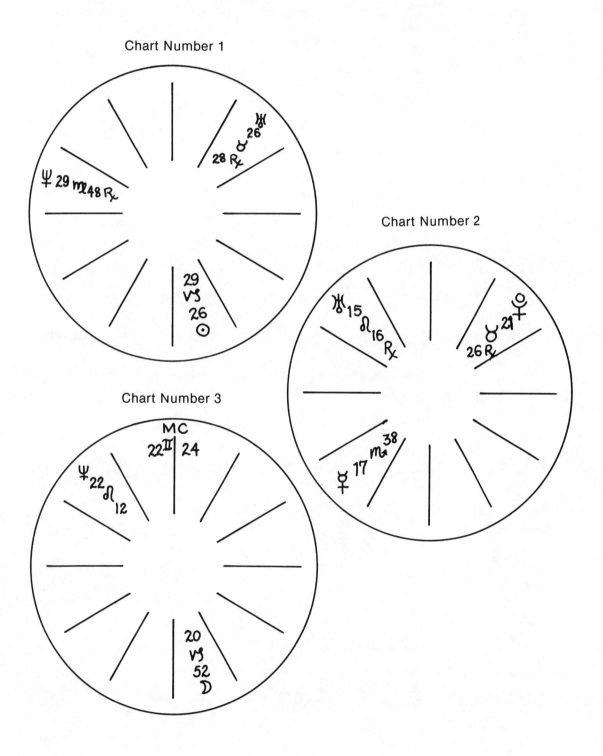

Chart Number 1

Chart Number 2

Chart Number 3

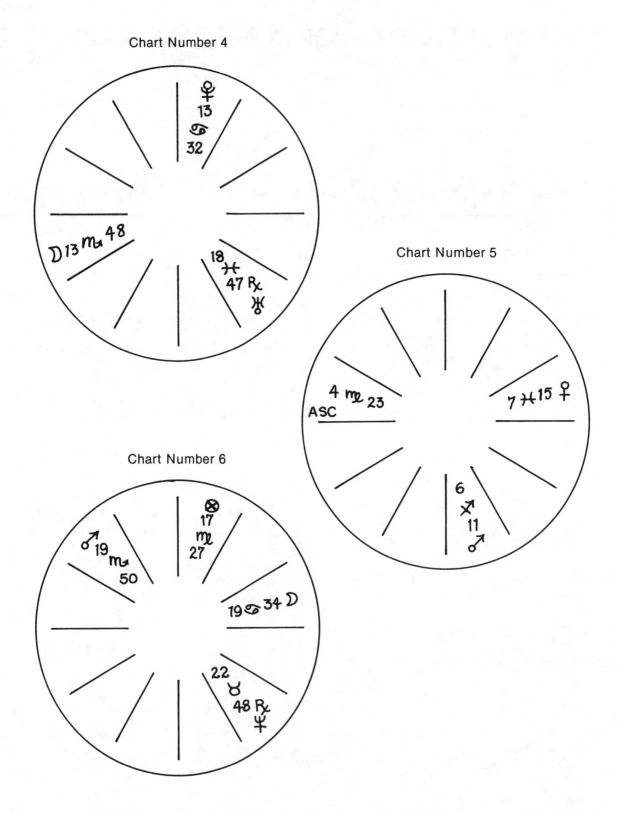

Chart Number 4

Chart Number 5

Chart Number 6

Homework Assignment

Major Configurations

A. Each of the charts contains a major configuration. Place the correct chart number next to each configuration listed below.

1. A Grand Trine in
   Water _____

2. A Yod _____

3. A Grand Trine in
   Earth _____

4. A fixed T-Square _____

5. A Cradle _____

6. A mutable T-Square _____

B. Below are possible manifestations of each major configuration. Place the correct chart number next to each description.

1. Help will come from outside. This individual will be standing in the right place, at the right time, at some point in his or her life._____

2. There will be a definite change at some point in this individual's life._____

3. This person may have the stick-to-it-iveness to overcome obstacles in life. He or she could also be stubborn._____

4. This person will be practical and may receive "gains"during his or her lifetime._____

5. This individual will be adaptable or changeable. When obstacles or problems appear, there might be a floundering from one decision to another._____

6. The positive expression is empathy and sympathy; the negative is that emotions may "run away" with this individual._____

5

WORKSHEET

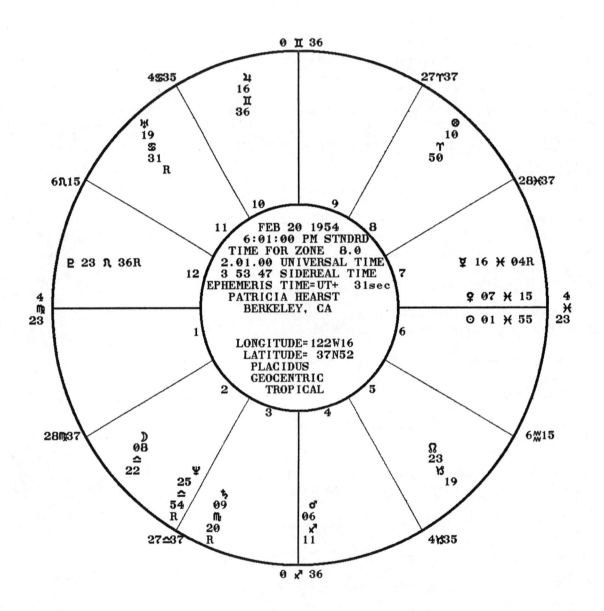

0 ♊ 36

4♋35   ♃ 16 ♊ 36   27♈37

♅ 19 ♋ 31 R   ⊗ 10 ♈ 50

6♌15   28♓37

10   9

11   FEB 20 1954 8
6:01:00 PM STNDRD
TIME FOR ZONE 8.0
2.01.00 UNIVERSAL TIME
3 53 47 SIDEREAL TIME
EPHEMERIS TIME=UT+ 31sec
PATRICIA HEARST
BERKELEY, CA

LONGITUDE=122W16
LATITUDE= 37N52
PLACIDUS
GEOCENTRIC
TROPICAL

♇ 23 ♌ 36R   12   7   ☿ 16 ♓ 04R

♀ 07 ♓ 15

4♍23   1   6   ☉ 01 ♓ 55   4♓23

2   5

3   4

28♍37   6♒15

☽ 08 ♎ 22   ☊ 23 ♑ 19

☓ 25 ♎ 54 R   ♄ 09 ♏ 20 R   ♂ 06 ♐ 11

27♎37   4♑35

0 ♐ 36

28

Worksheet

Name **Patricia Hearst**

Sun ♓ ___ Moon ♎ ___ Ascendant ♍ ___ Stellium ♓ ___

Ascendant Ruler ☿ House **7** MC Ruler ☿ House **7**

Elements, by Sign:	by House:	Hemisphere Emphasis:
Fire ♀ ♂		East **6**
Earth **Asc**	☽ ☿ ☉ ♃	West **4**
Air ♃ ☽ ♆ MC	♄ ♀ ☿ ♅	South **5**
Water ♅ ♄ ☊ ♀ ☿	♂ ♇	North **5**

Modes:		Polarity:
Cardinal ♅ ☽ ♆	♂ ♀ ☿ ♃	Positive **5**
Fixed ♇ ♄	☽ ♆ ♅	Negative **5**
Mutable ♃ ♂ ☊ ♀ ☿ MC A	♄ ☉ ♇	Temperament Pattern:

Sign Emphasis: ♓ ♑ ♎ **Splashish-bucketish**

Domal Planets _____ Mutual Reception ♀/♆ ☿/♃

Most Elevated Planet ♃ Planet Rising ☿

Planet Rising before ☉ ♂ Planet Last Conjuncted by ☽ ♇

Major Configurations, etc.:

Mutable Grand Cross

Cardinal T-Square

Grand Trine in Water

Homework Assignment

Patricia Hearst

1.   The Sun, Moon and Ascendant comprise the core of the individual. Note the signs these are in, and write a few sentences
or a list of key words that might describe Patricia Hearst.

II.   With the use of planets, points, signs, houses and aspects,
answer the following questions.

A. Patricia Hearst has a need for other people. Give at
least three reasons why.

B.   What in the chart tells you that she is very emotional?
Give at least three reasons.

C.   What tells you that she is very adaptable? Give at
least three reasons.

6

INTERPRETATION

Interpreting a Chart

There are many approaches to interpreting a chart, and the following approach is only one. The emphasis should always be on integrating the chart and visualizing it holistically, rather than concentrating on a single point or aspect.

Step 1. After the chart is erected, a work sheet including both general and specific information would be filled out. All of this material will be included in the interpretation.

Step 2. General qualities and the personality are usually examined first. The following should be included in a discussion of the personality, although not necessarily in this order:
   a. The signs of the Sun, Moon and Ascendant
   b. temperament pattern and hemisphere emphasis
   c. Element and mode emphases by sign and house
   d. Sign emphasis by sign and house
   e. Stelliums (if any)
   f. Planets conjunct the MC and Ascendant (if any)
   g. Characteristics of the signs in the first house
   h. Planets in the first house (if any) and how they are aspected
   i. Ruler(s) of the first house, where it is located and how it is aspected (there could be a co-ruler)
   j. Planet rising before the Sun
   k. Planet last conjuncted by the Moon
   l. Number of planets in positive and negative signs
   m. Mutual reception (if any)
   n. Major configurations discussed generally in terms of the signs, aspects and planets involved.

Step 3. Once the general personality is interpreted, any area of the life may be investigated. Again we start with the general and move to the specific.

    a. Determine which house or houses represent the area to be investigated.

    b. Note the signs contained in the house and combine the characteristics of the signs. These give the basic requirements of the individual in that area.

    c. If there are any planets or points (Node or Part of Fortune) in the house, they will provide more specific requirements in the area.

    d. Then, if the planets or points in the house are connected to a major configuration, the possible expression of the configuration in that area should be discussed.

    e. All other aspects to the planets or points in the house should be integrated with the major configurations for a more complete picture.

    f. Next, locate the ruler of the cusp of the house. There is a connection between the house being interpreted and the house in which its ruler is located.

    g. Note aspects to the house ruler for even more specific information about the house being investigated.

    h. If any particular planet might add to the understanding of the area, the planet's sign, house position and aspects should be added to the total picture. (E.g., Venus, the planet of love, might add information to the house of marriage.)

Some areas that usually seem of interest to the individual, and that would be included in any general interpretation are career, partnerships and the home (origins). There is no specific order in which these areas should be investigated.

Career discussion would include:

1. Signs in the tenth house
2. Planets and points in the tenth house and how they are aspected
3. Planet ruling the tenth house, where it is posited and how it is aspected
4. The sixth house represents daily work, so examining the sixth house in the same manner as the tenth (1-3 above) will provide information supplemental to career requirements
5. The second house represents, among other things, how one earns a living, so it can also supplement the career information
6. Always keep in mind, when investigating any area,

the general qualities of the personality because the personality will influence the direction of that area. For instance, if a person needs people you would not tell him to work alone, even if this is a professional possibility.

Partnership discussion would include:
1. Signs in the seventh house
2. Planets and points in the seventh house and how they are aspected.
3. Planet ruling the seventh house, where it is posited and how it is aspected
4. Fifth house if the partnership is a marriage, in the same manner as the seventh (1-3 above) but for courtships
5. Eighth house if the partnership is a marriage in the same manner as the seventh (1-3 above) but for sex and partner's resources
6 Venus (planet of love) for marriage—its house position, sign and aspects will give added information
7. Mars (sexual expression) for marriage—its house position, sign and aspects will give added information

Home discussion would include:
1. Signs in the fourth house
2. Planets and points in the fourth house and how they are aspected
3. Planet ruling the fourth house, where it is posited and how it is aspected

The relevant factors for other areas that might be discussed are:

Communications—Third and ninth houses, Mercury and Jupiter

Finances—second house (own resources and earning capacity) and eighth house (others' resources, inheritance)

Health—sixth house (physical health) and twelfth house (mental health)

Social Interaction—eleventh house (group participation) and seventh house (close one-to-one relations), location by sign and house of the Nodes and aspects to them

Children—fifth house for one's children generally and specifically one's first child, seventh for the second child, ninth, the third, etc.

REINFORCEMENT

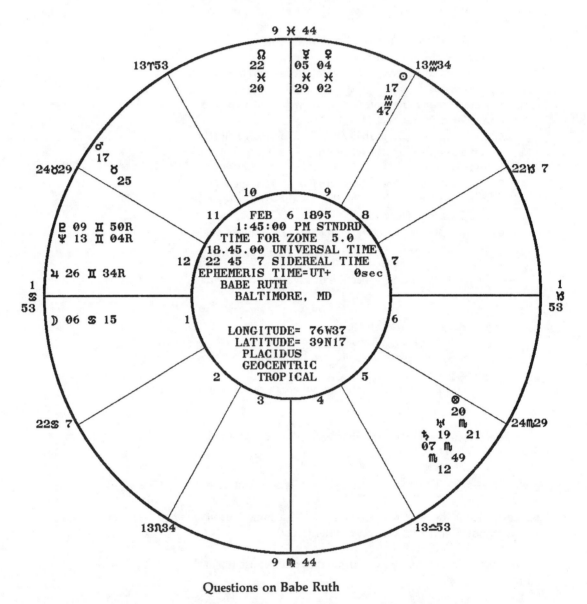

Questions on Babe Ruth

1. Babe Ruth was an individualist. Give two astrological reasons for this statement.

2. He was also a moody person. Give at least two astrological reasons for this assertion.

3. What major configuration might indicate that he had a violent temper which could erupt suddenly?

4. There are a number of astrological reasons for the fact that he was a great baseball player—one of which was the positive manifestation of the major configuration mentioned in 3 above. Using the planets, signs and houses involved in this configuration, explain why.

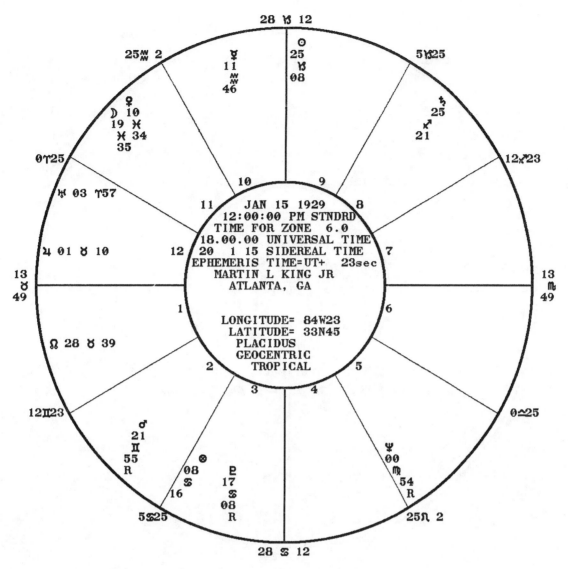

28 ♑ 12

25 ♒ 2

☿ 11 ♒ 46

☉ 25 ♑ 08

5 ♓ 25

♀ 10 ♓ 34

☽ 19 ♓ 35

♄ 25 ♐ 21

0 ♈ 25

♅ 03 ♈ 57

12 ♐ 23

10

9

11

12

♃ 01 ♉ 10

8

JAN 15 1929
12:00:00 PM STNDRD
TIME FOR ZONE   6.0
18.00.00 UNIVERSAL TIME
20 1 15 SIDEREAL TIME
EPHEMERIS TIME=UT+   23sec
MARTIN L KING JR
ATLANTA, GA

LONGITUDE= 84W23
LATITUDE= 33N45
PLACIDUS
GEOCENTRIC
TROPICAL

7

13 ♉ 49

13 ♏ 49

Ω 28 ♉ 39

1

6

12 ♊ 23

2

5

♂ 21 ♊ 55 R

3

4

0 ♎ 25

⊗ 08 ♋ 16

♇ 17 ♋ 08 R

♆ 00 ♍ 54 R

25 ♌ 2

5 ♋ 25

28 ♋ 12

5. Would he look for a partner to provide stability or freedom? Why?

6. Give three astrological indications that he might be proficient in sports.

Questions on Martin Luther King, Jr.

1. Considering the signs of his Sun, Moon and Ascendant, tell which would explain the following characteristics.

     a. He was conservative. _____
     b. He could be stubborn or persistent. _____
     c. He was ambitious. _____
     d. He felt deeply for people. _____
     e. He was goal-oriented. _____
     f. He "had a dream." _____
     g. He often responded emotionally._____
     h. His resistance was "non-violent." _____

2. Why would speeches and writing be particularly important in his career?

3. What indicates that he might find ego satisfaction through religion?

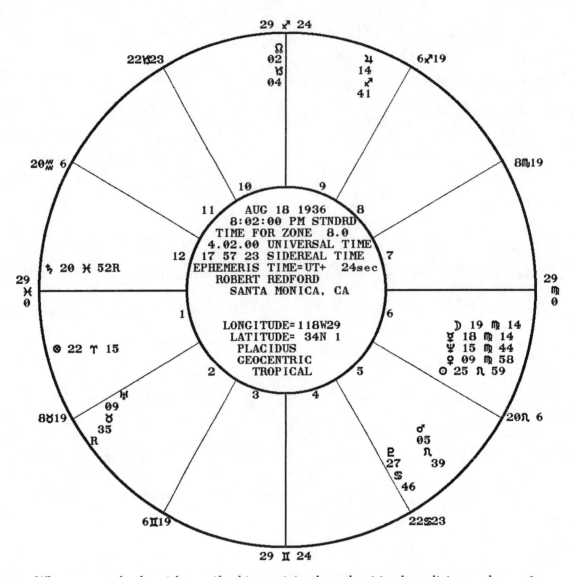

29 ♐ 24

22♑23

20 ≈ 6

29 ♓ 0

♄ 20 ♓ 52R

⊗ 22 ♈ 15

8♉19

♅ 09 ♉ 35 R

6♊19

29 ♊ 24

☊ 02 ♑ 04

♃ 14 ♐ 41

6♐19

8♏19

AUG 18 1936
8:02:00 PM STNDRD
TIME FOR ZONE 8.0
4.02.00 UNIVERSAL TIME
17 57 23 SIDEREAL TIME
EPHEMERIS TIME=UT+ 24sec
ROBERT REDFORD
SANTA MONICA, CA

LONGITUDE= 118W29
LATITUDE= 34N 1
PLACIDUS
GEOCENTRIC
TROPICAL

29 ♏ 0

☽ 19 ♏ 14
☿ 18 ♏ 14
♆ 15 ♏ 44
♀ 09 ♏ 58
☉ 25 ♌ 59

20♌ 6

♂ 05 ♌ 39

♇ 27 ♋ 46

22♋23

4. What suggests that he might manifest his creativity through spiritual or religious endeavors?

5. Using houses, signs and planets, describe why he was involved with equality of groups. Be sure to include astrological reasons for his deep emotional involvement with this cause.

Questions on Robert Redford

1. Consider only the signs of the Sun, Moon and Ascendant, and state which would indicate the following characteristics.

     a.   Acting ability. _____

     b.   Sensitivity to others. _____

     c.   Interest in detail. _____

     d.   Criticalness. _____

     e.   Self-sacrificingness. _____

     f.   "Outgoingness". _____

2. What might tell you that he could have difficulty dealing with abstract ideas?

3. What would tell you that he has traveled a great deal?

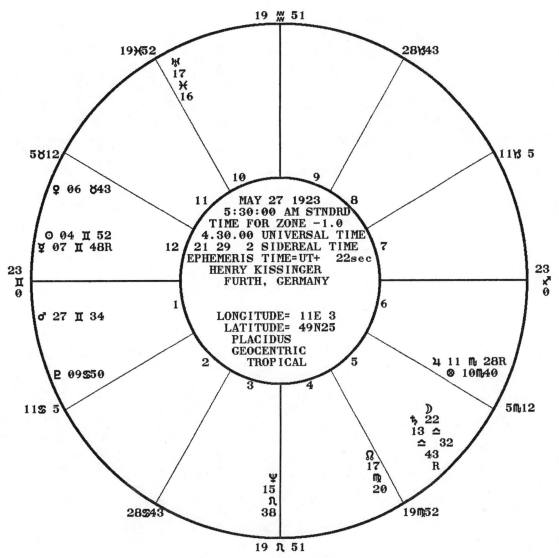

19 ≈ 51

19⌐52   28⅓43

♄ 17 ⅘ 16

5♉12   11⅓ 5

♀ 06 ♉43

☉ 04 ♊ 52
☿ 07 ♊ 48R   23
                              ✗
23   0
♊
0

♂ 27 ♊ 34   6

♇ 09♋50   ♃ 11 ♏ 28R
                        ⊗ 10♏40

11♋ 5   5♏12

☽ 22
♄ 13 ♎
♎ 32
☊ 43
17 R
♏ 20

Ψ 15 ♌ 38

28♋43   19♏52

19 ♌ 51

MAY 27 1923
5:30:00 AM STNDRD
TIME FOR ZONE −1.0
4.30.00 UNIVERSAL TIME
21 29 2 SIDEREAL TIME
EPHEMERIS TIME=UT+   22sec
HENRY KISSINGER
FURTH, GERMANY

LONGITUDE= 11E 3
LATITUDE= 49N25
PLACIDUS
GEOCENTRIC
TROPICAL

4.   As a young man, he reportedly was a drifter and drinker. Explain why in terms of a major configuration in his chart. In your explanation use the mode, planets, signs and aspects involved.

5.   When he met his wife, his life began to stabilize. This change can be explained as a positive manifestation of the same configuration. Why and how? In your explanation again utilize the mode, planets, signs and aspects.

Questions on Henry Kissinger

1.   There are a number of indications that Henry Kissinger's mental qualities are of very special importance. Give three. Your answer should include signs, major configurations and planets.

2.   What signs, emphasized in this chart, would show that he might be a good mediator?

3.   What tells you that he is a dynamic, hard-driving person?

4.   What major configuration demonstrates that he may be highly emotional?

5.   What planet in which house shows that there might be changes in his career?

6.   Describe the type of person he might seek as a marriage partner.

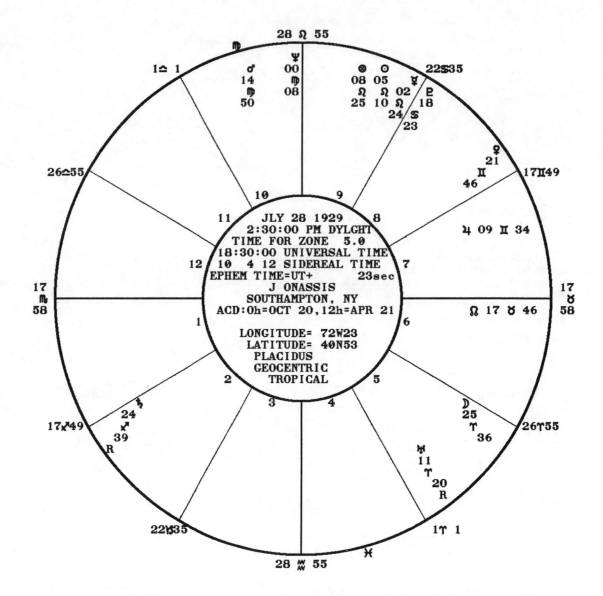

Questions on Jacqueline Onassis

1.   Using the signs of her Sun, Moon and Ascendant, explain why she tries to avoid publicity, and yet often finds herself the center of attention.

2.   What is the astrological evidence of her proficiency in French?

3.   What indicates her charisma?

4.   What is she looking for in a partner?

5.   What are the astrological indications that she could inherit a large amount of money and that this money might come from a partner?

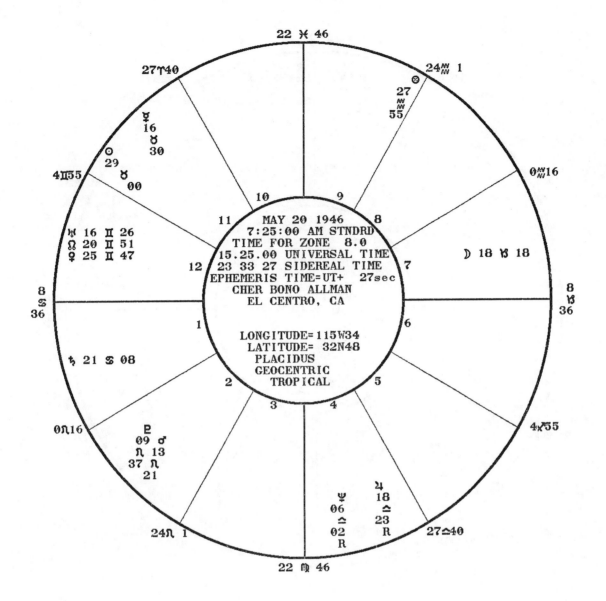

22 ♓ 46

27♈40

24♒ 1

27 ♒ 55

⊗

☿ 16 ♉ 30

☉ 29 ♉ 00

0♒16

4♊55

♅ 16 ♊ 26
☊ 20 ♊ 51
♀ 25 ♊ 47

10

11

9

8

MAY 20 1946
7:25:00 AM STNDRD
TIME FOR ZONE 8.0
15.25.00 UNIVERSAL TIME
23 33 27 SIDEREAL TIME
EPHEMERIS TIME=UT+ 27sec
CHER BONO ALLMAN
EL CENTRO, CA

LONGITUDE=115W34
LATITUDE= 32N48
PLACIDUS
GEOCENTRIC
TROPICAL

☽ 18 ♑ 18

7

12

8 ♋ 36

1

8 ♑ 36

♄ 21 ♋ 08

6

2

5

0♌16

♇ 09 ♌ 13
♂ 37 ♌ 21

3

4

4♐55

♆ 06 ♎ 02 R

♃ 18 ♎ 23 R

27♎40

24♌ 1

22 ♍ 46

Questions on Cher Bono Allman

1. What are the astrological indications of her musical ability?

2. What would disclose that she might be a basically shy person?

3. Why does she have a strong interdependence with a partner?

4. Using a major configuration in the chart explain the kind of problem that might arise because of this interdependency.

5. How could this problem be alleviated?

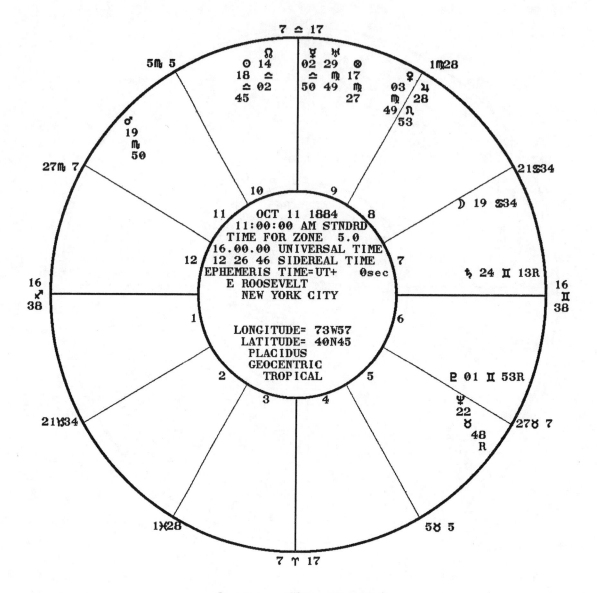

Questions on Eleanor Roosevelt

1. Consider only the signs of her Sun, Moon and Ascendant, and tell which would explain the following characteristics.

> a. Deep feeling in a motherly sense. _____
> b. Outspokenness. _____
> c. Love of distant travel. _____
> d. Home-orientation. _____
> e. Diplomacy. _____
> f. Need for harmony. _____

2. Why would her opportunities usually come from others?

3. What indicates that she developed mainly through experience?

4. She did a great deal of world traveling. Give three astrological reasons.

5. What would indicate that distant travel could be connected with her career?

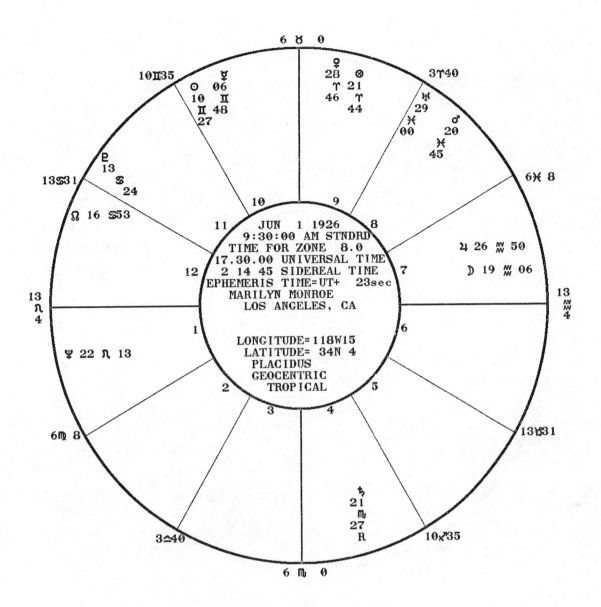

6Ⅱ35

10Ⅱ35

☿ 06
⊙ 10 Ⅱ
Ⅱ 48
27

♀ 28
⊗ ♈ 21
♈ 46
♈ 44

3♈40

♅ 29
♓ 00

♂ 20
♓ 45

6♓8

♇ 13
♋ 24

13♋31

Ω 16 ♋53

10

9

8

11   JUN 1 1926
9:30:00 AM STNDRD
TIME FOR ZONE 8.0
17.30.00 UNIVERSAL TIME
2 14 45 SIDEREAL TIME
EPHEMERIS TIME=UT+ 23sec
MARILYN MONROE
LOS ANGELES, CA

LONGITUDE= 118W15
LATITUDE= 34N 4
PLACIDUS
GEOCENTRIC
TROPICAL

12

7

♃ 26 ≈ 50

☽ 19 ≈ 06

13
≈
4

13
♌
4

1

6

♆ 22 ♌ 13

2

5

6♍ 8

3

4

3♎40

♄
21
♏
27
R

10♐35

13♑31

6♏ 0

6. What denotes that writing might also be associated with her career?

Questions on Marilyn Monroe

1. What in Marilyn Monroe's chart indicates that she was called a "sex goddess?"

2. Give five astrological reasons which verify that acting was a good career for her.

3. What would indicate that her emotions might "run away with her?"

4. What implies that her home was a restrictive area for her?

5. Using a major configuration in the chart, explain what kind of problem she could have had with her mother.

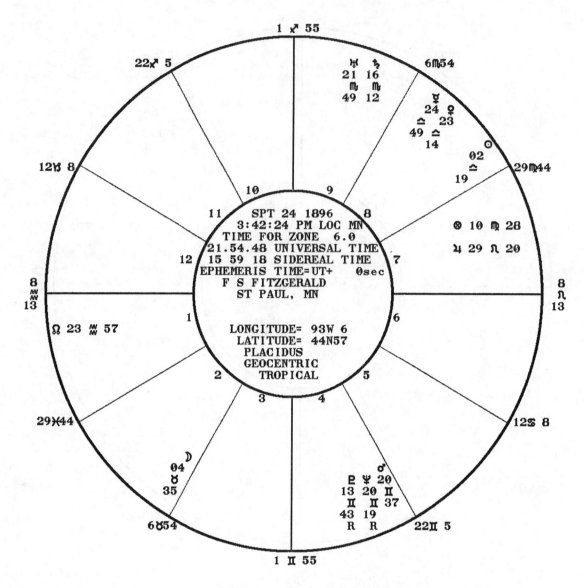

Questions on F. Scott Fitzgerald

1. Consider the signs of the Sun, Moon and Ascendant and tell which would explain the following characteristics.

      a. Individualism. _____

      b. Artistic ability. _____

      c. Need for freedom. _____

      d. Stubbornness. _____

      e. Partnership orientation. _____

      f. Desire to acquire material possessions. _____

2. What major configuration shows his ability to deal effectively with ideas and abstractions?

3. What major configuration indicates that he might have sudden changes in his relationships?

4. Give at least three astrological indications of his writing ability.

5. Why would distant travel appeal to him?

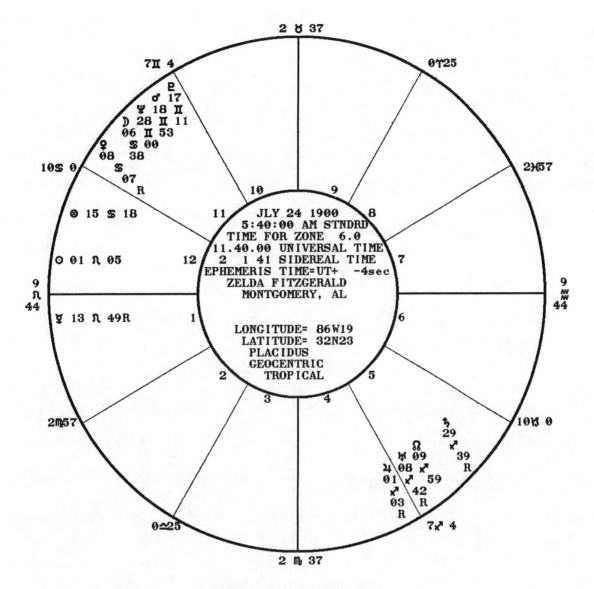

Questions on Zelda Fitzgerald

1. What indicates that Zelda Fitzgerald needed to balance some parts of her life with other parts?

2. She had an active social life. Give three astrological reasons for this activity.

3. In later life she found great solace in the spiritual. Explain this development astrologically.

4. Why would she feel most comfortable in a large, lavish home?

5. She wrote with an artistic flair and with deep feeling. This endeavor was important to her. Why was this so?

6. What was she looking for in a partner?

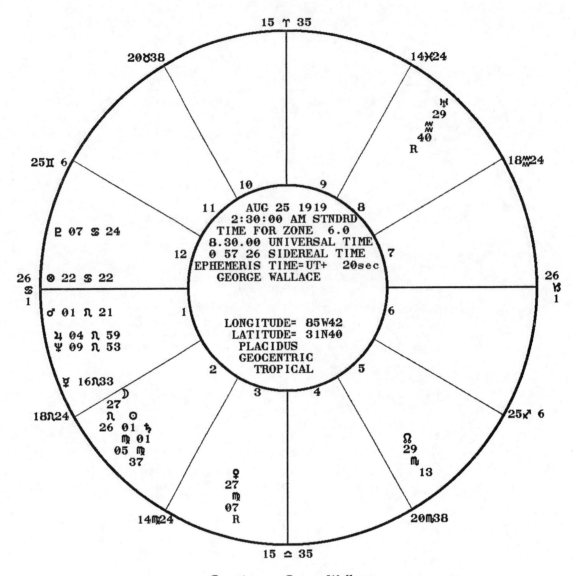

Questions on George Wallace

1. Does George Wallace adjust to the world, or does he adjust the world to him? Give the astrological reason.

2. Is he a person of broad or narrow interests? What is the astrological reason?

3. Give two astrological reasons to explain why he is an initiator.

4. Write a sentence on how each of the planets in his first house might manifest in his personality.

5. Is security important to him? Why or why not?

6. He has been called an effective speaker. Using the third house and Mercury, explain why.

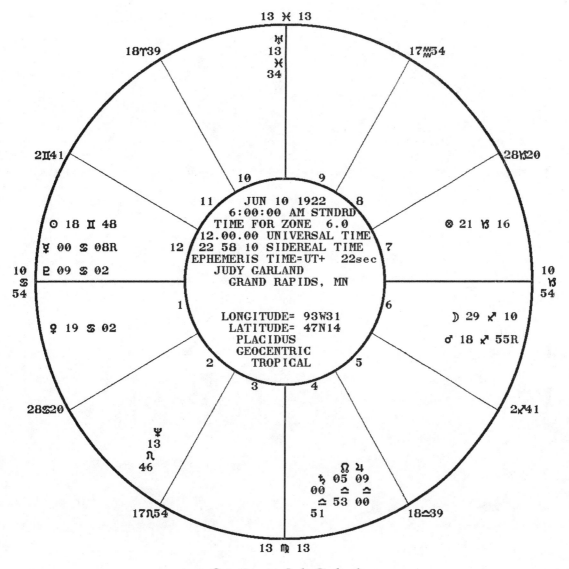

Questions on Judy Garland

1. Consider the signs of the Sun, Moon and Ascendant, and state which would explain the following characteristics.

      a. Outspokenness. _____

      b. Sociability. _____

      c. Love of travel. _____

      d. Nervousness. _____

      e. Moodiness. _____

      f. Great emotionality. _____

2. Having a partner was important for her sense of wholeness. Why?

3. What aspect indicates that she might have had a temper?

4. What indicates that this temper might have flared up suddenly?

5. There is a major configuration which shows that she could have had difficulty in partnerships. What is this configuration?

45

Calculation Form

1. Name: _____
   Source of Data: _____

2. Birthdate: _____

3. Birthplace: _____
   Longitude: _____ Latitude: _____

4. Birthtime (use 24-hour system):

   Daylight Saving Time (if applicable) ____ h ____ m ____ s

   Standard Time ____ h ____ m ____ s

   + *or* − hours from birthplace to Greenwich ____ h ____ m ____ s

   −24 if Greenwich Birthtime is over 24 hours ____ h ____ m ____ s

   Altered Birthdate if Greenwich Birthtime is over 24 hours _____

5. Local Sidereal Time:

   Sidereal Time ____ h ____ m ____ s

   + Greenwich Birthtime ____ h ____ m ____ s

   +9.86 seconds × Greenwich Birthtime ____ h ____ m ____ s

   = Greenwich Sidereal Time of Birth ____ h ____ m ____ s

   + or − Longitude Time Equivalent (E+, W−) ____ h ____ m ____ s

   = Local Sidereal Time of Birth ____ h ____ m ____ s

6. House Cusps:

   Sidereal Time Factor _____

   Latitude Factor _____

   10th (MC) ____ °

   11th ____ °

   12th ____ °

   1st (Asc.) ____ °

   2nd ____ °

   3rd ____ °

7. Planets and Points:

   Constant: _____

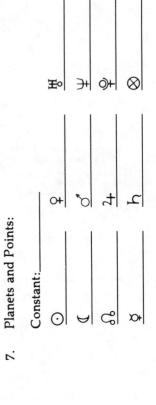

☉ ____	♀ ____	♅ ____
☽ ____	♂ ____	♆ ____
☊ ____	♃ ____	♇ ____
☿ ____	♄ ____	⊗ ____

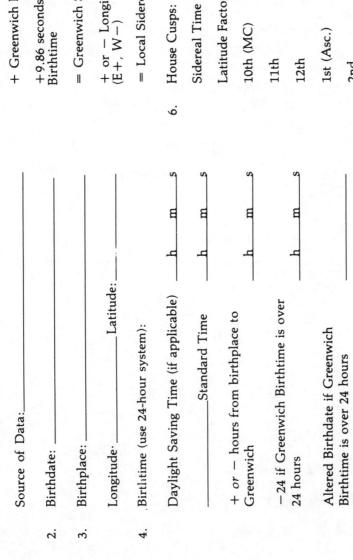

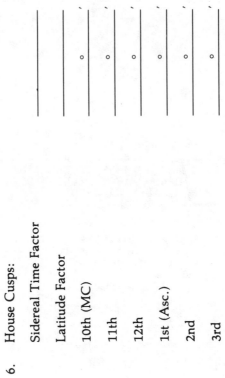

10th House Cusp (MC):

MC for later Sidereal Time _____° _____'

MC for earlier Sidereal Time _____° _____'

(Subtract) _____° _____' (a)

STF × (a) = _____° _____' (b)

Earlier MC _____° _____'

+ (b) _____° _____'

= MC _____° _____'

11th House Cusp:

11th for later Sidereal Time _____° _____'

11th for earlier Sidereal Time _____° _____'

(Subtract) _____° _____' (c)

STF × (c) = _____° _____' (d)

Larger house cusp _____° _____'

Smaller house cusp _____° _____'

(Subtract) = _____° _____' (e)

LF × (e) = _____° _____' (f)

Earlier 11th house cusp _____° _____'

+ (d) _____° _____'

+ or – (f) = 11th house cusp _____° _____'

12th House Cusp:

12th for later Sidereal Time _____° _____'

12th for earlier Sidereal Time _____° _____'

(Subtract) _____° _____' (g)

STF × (g) = _____° _____' (h)

Larger house cusp _____° _____'

Smaller house cusp _____° _____'

(Subtract) = _____° _____' (i)

LF × (i) = _____° _____' (j)

Earlier 12th house cusp _____° _____'

+ (h) _____° _____'

+ or – (j) = 12th house cusp _____° _____'

1st House Cusp (Asc.):

1st for later Sidereal Time _____° _____'

1st for earlier Sidereal Time _____° _____'

(Subtract) _____° _____' (k)

STF × (k) = _____° _____' (l)

Larger house cusp _____°_____'

Smaller house cusp _____°_____'

(Subtract) = (m) _____°_____'

LF × (m) = (n) _____°_____'

Earlier 1st house cusp _____°_____'

+ (l) = _____°_____'

+ or − (n) = 1st house cusp _____°_____'

2nd House Cusp

2nd for later Sidereal Time _____°_____'

2nd for earlier Sidereal Time _____°_____'

(Subtract) (o) _____°_____'

STF × (o) = (p) _____°_____'

Larger house cusp _____°_____'

Smaller house cusp _____°_____'

(Subtract) = (q) _____°_____'

LF × (q) = (r) _____°_____'

Earlier 2nd house cusp _____°_____'

+ (p) = _____°_____'

+ or − (r) = 2nd house cusp _____°_____'

3rd House Cusp:

3rd for later Sidereal Time _____°_____'

3rd for earlier Sidereal Time _____°_____'

(Subtract) (s) _____°_____'

STF × (s) = (t) _____°_____'

Larger house cusp _____°_____'

Smaller house cusp _____°_____'

(Subtract) = (u) _____°_____'

LF × (u) = (v) _____°_____'

Earlier 3rd house cusp _____°_____'

+ (t) = _____°_____'

+ or − (v) = 3rd house cusp _____°_____'

48

Calculation of Planets

Constant = [(Minutes of Greenwich Birthtime ÷ 60) + Hours of Greenwich Birthtime] ÷ 24

Constant = _____

☉ (Always moves forward)

Position for later date _____ °

Position for earlier date _____ °

Distance traveled _____ ° ' "

× Constant _____ ° ' " = (a)

Earlier position _____ ° ' "

+ (a) _____ ° ' " = Birth position ☉

☽ (Always moves forward)

Position for later date _____ °

Position for earlier date _____ °

Distance traveled _____ ° ' "

× Constant _____ ° ' " = (b)

Earlier position _____ ° ' "

+ (b) _____ ° ' " = Birth position ☽

☊ (Always moves backward)

Position for later date _____ °

Position for earlier date _____ °

Distance traveled _____ ° '

× Constant _____ = (c)

Earlier position _____ ° '

− (c) _____ = Birth position ☊

☿ (May move forward or backward)

Larger _____ ° '

Smaller _____ ° '

Distance traveled _____

× Constant _____ = (d)

Earlier position _____ ° '

+ or − (d) _____ = Birth position ☿

♀ (May move forward or backward)

Larger _____ ° '

Smaller _____ ° '

Distance traveled _____

× Constant _____ = (e)

Earlier position _____ ° '

+ or − (e) _____ = Birth position ♀

♂ (May move forward or backward)

Larger _____ ° '

Smaller _____ ° '

Distance traveled _____ ° '

× Constant _____ = (f)

Earlier position _____ ° '

♂
+ or − (f) _____ ° ____ ' = Birth position

♃ (May move forward or backward)
Larger _____ ° ____ '
Smaller _____ ° ____ '
Distance traveled _____ ° ____ '
× Constant _____ ° ____ ' = (g)
Earlier position _____ ° ____ '
+ or − (g) _____ ° ____ ' = Birth position

♄ (May move forward or backward)
Larger _____ ° ____ '
Smaller _____ ° ____ '
Distance traveled _____ ° ____ '
× Constant _____ ° ____ ' = (h)
Earlier position _____ ° ____ '
+ or − (h) _____ ° ____ ' = Birth position

♅ (May move forward or backward)
Larger _____ ° ____ '
Smaller _____ ° ____ '
Distance traveled _____ ° ____ '
× Constant _____ ° ____ ' = (i)
Earlier position _____ ° ____ '
+ or − (i) _____ ° ____ ' = Birth position

♆ (May move forward or backward)
Larger _____ ° ____ '
Smaller _____ ° ____ '
Distance traveled _____ ° ____ '
× Constant _____ ° ____ ' = (j)
Earlier position _____ ° ____ '
+ or − (j) _____ ° ____ ' = Birth position

♇ (May move forward or backward)
Larger _____ ° ____ '
Smaller _____ ° ____ '
Distance traveled _____ ° ____ '
× Constant _____ ° ____ ' = (k)
Earlier position _____ ° ____ '
+ or − (k) _____ ° ____ ' = Birth position

⊗ Part of Fortune (enter signs by number, e.g., Aries, 1; Taurus, 2; etc.)
Ascendant _____ ° ____ '
+ Moon _____ ° ____ '
= _____ ° ____ '
− Sun _____ ° ____ '
= Part of Fortune _____ ° ____ '

Placidus Table of Houses for Latitudes 0° to 60° North

3h 44m 0s — 56° 0' 0" — 28 ♉ 15

LAT.	11	12	ASC	2	3
0	26♊20	24♋ 6	23♌41	25♍38	28♎ 0
5	27 0	25 20	24 53	25 45	27 40
10	27 40	26 33	26 3	25 51	27 20
15	28 22	27 46	27 11	25 57	27 0
20	29 6	29 2	28 18	26 3	26 40
21	29 16	29 17	28 31	26 5	26 36
22	29 25	29 33	28 45	26 6	26 32
23	29 34	29 49	28 58	26 7	26 27
24	29 44	0♌ 5	29 11	26 8	26 23
25	29 54	0 21	29 25	26 10	26 19
26	0♋ 4	0 37	29 38	26 11	26 14
27	0 14	0 54	29 52	26 12	26 10
28	0 24	1 10	0♍ 6	26 13	26 5
29	0 35	1 27	0 19	26 15	26 1
30	0 46	1 44	0 33	26 16	25 56
31	0 57	2 2	0 47	26 17	25 52
32	1 8	2 19	1 1	26 18	25 47
33	1 20	2 37	1 15	26 20	25 42
34	1 32	2 56	1 29	26 21	25 37
35	1 44	3 14	1 43	26 22	25 32
36	1 57	3 33	1 57	26 24	25 27
37	2 10	3 52	2 12	26 25	25 22
38	2 23	4 12	2 26	26 27	25 16
39	2 37	4 32	2 41	26 28	25 11
40	2 51	4 53	2 56	26 29	25 5
41	3 5	5 14	3 11	26 31	25 0
42	3 21	5 35	3 27	26 32	24 54
43	3 36	5 57	3 42	26 34	24 48
44	3 53	6 20	3 58	26 36	24 42
45	4 10	6 43	4 14	26 37	24 36
46	4 28	7 7	4 30	26 39	24 29
47	4 46	7 31	4 47	26 40	24 23
48	5 6	7 56	5 4	26 42	24 16
49	5 26	8 22	5 21	26 44	24 9
50	5 47	8 49	5 38	26 45	24 1
51	6 10	9 16	5 56	26 47	23 54
52	6 33	9 45	6 14	26 49	23 46
53	6 58	10 14	6 32	26 51	23 38
54	7 25	10 45	6 51	26 53	23 30
55	7 53	11 16	7 11	26 55	23 21
56	8 24	11 49	7 30	26 57	23 12
57	8 56	12 23	7 51	26 59	23 3
58	9 31	12 58	8 11	27 1	22 53
59	10 9	13 35	8 33	27 3	22 42
60	10♋50	14♌13	8♍54	27♍ 6	22♎32

3h 48m 0s — 57° 0' 0" — 29 ♉ 13

LAT.	11	12	ASC	2	3
0	27♊15	25♋ 3	24♌42	26♍44	29♎ 3
5	27 55	26 16	25 54	26 49	28 42
10	28 35	27 28	27 2	26 53	28 22
15	29 17	28 42	28 8	26 58	28 1
20	0♋ 2	29 56	29 13	27 3	27 40
21	0 11	0♌12	29 26	27 3	27 36
22	0 20	0 27	29 39	27 4	27 32
23	0 29	0 43	29 52	27 5	27 27
24	0 39	0 59	0♍ 5	27 6	27 23
25	0 49	1 15	0 18	27 7	27 18
26	0 59	1 31	0 31	27 8	27 14
27	1 9	1 47	0 44	27 9	27 9
28	1 19	2 4	0 58	27 10	27 5
29	1 30	2 20	1 11	27 11	27 0
30	1 41	2 37	1 24	27 12	26 55
31	1 52	2 54	1 38	27 13	26 50
32	2 3	3 12	1 51	27 14	26 45
33	2 15	3 30	2 5	27 15	26 40
34	2 27	3 48	2 19	27 16	26 35
35	2 39	4 6	2 32	27 17	26 30
36	2 51	4 25	2 46	27 18	26 25
37	3 4	4 44	3 0	27 19	26 19
38	3 18	5 3	3 15	27 20	26 14
39	3 31	5 23	3 29	27 21	26 8
40	3 45	5 43	3 44	27 22	26 3
41	4 0	6 4	3 58	27 23	25 57
42	4 15	6 25	4 13	27 24	25 51
43	4 31	6 47	4 28	27 25	25 44
44	4 47	7 9	4 44	27 27	25 38
45	5 4	7 32	4 59	27 28	25 32
46	5 22	7 56	5 15	27 29	25 25
47	5 40	8 20	5 31	27 30	25 18
48	6 0	8 45	5 47	27 31	25 11
49	6 20	9 10	6 4	27 33	25 4
50	6 41	9 36	6 21	27 34	24 56
51	7 3	10 3	6 38	27 35	24 48
52	7 27	10 31	6 56	27 37	24 40
53	7 52	11 0	7 14	27 38	24 32
54	8 18	11 30	7 32	27 40	24 23
55	8 46	12 1	7 51	27 41	24 14
56	9 16	12 33	8 10	27 43	24 5
57	9 49	13 7	8 30	27 44	23 55
58	10 23	13 41	8 50	27 46	23 45
59	11 1	14 17	9 10	27 48	23 34
60	11♋41	14♌55	9♍31	27♍49	23♎23

3h 52m 0s — 58° 0' 0" — 0 ♊ 11

LAT.	11	12	ASC	2	3
0	28♊10	26♋ 0	25♌44	27♍49	0♏ 6
5	28 50	27 12	26 54	27 52	29♎45
10	29 30	28 24	28 0	27 56	29 24
15	0♋12	29 37	29 5	27 59	29 2
20	0 57	0♌51	0♍ 8	28 2	28 41
21	1 6	1 6	0 21	28 2	28 36
22	1 15	1 22	0 33	28 3	28 32
23	1 24	1 37	0 46	28 4	28 27
24	1 34	1 53	0 59	28 4	28 23
25	1 44	2 8	1 11	28 5	28 18
26	1 54	2 24	1 24	28 5	28 13
27	2 4	2 40	1 37	28 6	28 8
28	2 14	2 57	1 50	28 7	28 4
29	2 25	3 13	2 3	28 7	27 59
30	2 36	3 30	2 16	28 8	27 54
31	2 47	3 47	2 29	28 9	27 49
32	2 58	4 4	2 42	28 9	27 44
33	3 10	4 22	2 55	28 10	27 39
34	3 21	4 40	3 8	28 11	27 33
35	3 34	4 58	3 22	28 11	27 28
36	3 46	5 16	3 35	28 12	27 22
37	3 59	5 35	3 49	28 13	27 17
38	4 12	5 55	4 3	28 13	27 11
39	4 26	6 14	4 17	28 14	27 5
40	4 40	6 34	4 31	28 15	26 59
41	4 55	6 55	4 45	28 15	26 53
42	5 10	7 16	5 0	28 16	26 47
43	5 25	7 37	5 15	28 17	26 41
44	5 42	7 59	5 29	28 18	26 34
45	5 58	8 21	5 44	28 19	26 28
46	6 16	8 45	6 0	28 19	26 21
47	6 34	9 8	6 15	28 20	26 13
48	6 54	9 33	6 31	28 21	26 6
49	7 14	9 58	6 47	28 22	25 59
50	7 35	10 24	7 4	28 23	25 51
51	7 57	10 50	7 20	28 24	25 43
52	8 20	11 18	7 38	28 25	25 34
53	8 45	11 46	7 55	28 25	25 26
54	9 11	12 16	8 13	28 26	25 17
55	9 39	12 46	8 31	28 27	25 7
56	10 9	13 18	8 49	28 28	24 58
57	10 41	13 51	9 8	28 29	24 48
58	11 15	14 25	9 28	28 31	24 37
59	11 52	15 0	9 48	28 32	24 26
60	12♋32	15♌37	10♍ 8	28♍33	24♎14

3h 56m 0s — 59° 0' 0" — 1 ♊ 8

LAT.	11	12	ASC	2	3
0	29♊ 5	26♋57	26♌47	28♍55	1♏ 8
5	29 45	28 9	27 54	28 56	0 47
10	0♋25	29 20	28 59	28 58	0 25
15	1 7	0♌32	0♍ 2	28 59	0 3
20	1 52	1 46	1 3	29 1	29♎41
21	2 1	2 1	1 16	29 1	29 36
22	2 10	2 16	1 28	29 1	29 31
23	2 19	2 31	1 40	29 2	29 27
24	2 29	2 47	1 52	29 2	29 22
25	2 39	3 2	2 5	29 2	29. 17
26	2 49	3 18	2 17	29 3	29 12
27	2 59	3 34	2 30	29 3	29 8
28	3 9	3 50	2 42	29 3	29 3
29	3 20	4 6	2 55	29 4	28 58
30	3 30	4 23	3 7	29 4	28 53
31	3 41	4 40	3 20	29 4	28 47
32	3 53	4 57	3 33	29 5	28 42
33	4 4	5 14	3 46	29 5	28 37
34	4 16	5 32	3 58	29 5	28 31
35	4 28	5 50	4 11	29 6	28 26
36	4 41	6 8	4 25	29 6	28 20
37	4 54	6 27	4 38	29 6	28 14
38	5 7	6 46	4 51	29 7	28 9
39	5 20	7 5	5 5	29 7	28 3
40	5 34	7 25	5 19	29 7	27 56
41	5 49	7 45	5 32	29 8	27 50
42	6 4	8 6	5 46	29 8	27 44
43	6 20	8 27	6 1	29 8	27 37
44	6 36	8 48	6 15	29 9	27 30
45	6 53	9 11	6 30	29 9	27 23
46	7 10	9 33	6 45	29 10	27 16
47	7 28	9 57	7 0	29 10	27 9
48	7 48	10 21	7 15	29 10	27 1
49	8 8	10 46	7 31	29 11	26 53
50	8 28	11 11	7 47	29 11	26 45
51	8 51	11 37	8 3	29 12	26 37
52	9 14	12 4	8 19	29 12	26 28
53	9 38	12 32	8 36	29 13	26 19
54	10 4	13 1	8 53	29 13	26 10
55	10 32	13 31	9 11	29 14	26 0
56	11 2	14 3	9 29	29 14	25 50
57	11 33	14 35	9 47	29 15	25 40
58	12 7	15 8	10 6	29 15	25 29
59	12 44	15 43	10 26	29 16	25 18
60	13♋23	16♌19	10♍46	29♍16	25♎ 6

4h 0m 0s — 60° 0' 0" — 2 ♊ 5

LAT.	11	12	ASC	2	3
0	0♋ 0	27♋55	27♌49	30♍ 0	2♏11
5	0 40	29 6	28 55	0♎ 0	1 49
10	1 20	0♌16	29 58	30♍ 0	1 26
15	2 2	1 28	0♍59	0♎ 0	1 4
20	2 46	2 40	1 58	30♍ 0	0 41
21	2 56	2 55	2 10	30 0	0 36
22	3 5	3 10	2 22	30 0	0 31
23	3 14	3 25	2 34	30 0	0 26
24	3 24	3 41	2 46	30 0	0 22
25	3 34	3 56	2 58	30 0	0 17
26	3 44	4 12	3 10	0♎ 0	0 12
27	3 54	4 27	3 22	0 0	0 7
28	4 4	4 43	3 34	0 0	0 1
29	4 14	5 0	3 47	0 0	29♎56
30	4 25	5 16	3 59	0 0	29 51
31	4 36	5 33	4 11	0 0	29 46
32	4 47	5 50	4 23	30♍ 0	29 40
33	4 59	6 7	4 36	30 0	29 35
34	5 11	6 24	4 48	30 0	29 29
35	5 23	6 42	5 1	30 0	29 23
36	5 35	7 0	5 14	30 0	29 18
37	5 48	7 18	5 27	0♎ 0	29 12
38	6 1	7 37	5 40	0 0	29 6
39	6 15	7 56	5 53	0 0	29 0
40	6 29	8 15	6 6	0 0	28 53
41	6 43	8 35	6 20	30♍ 0	28 47
42	6 58	8 56	6 33	30 0	28 40
43	7 14	9 17	6 47	30 0	28 33
44	7 30	9 38	7 1	30 0	28 26
45	7 47	10 0	7 15	0♎ 0	28 19
46	8 4	10 22	7 29	0 0	28 12
47	8 22	10 45	7 44	0 0	28 4
48	8 41	11 9	7 59	30♍ 0	27 56
49	9 1	11 33	8 14	30 0	27 48
50	9 22	11 58	8 29	0♎ 0	27 40
51	9 44	12 24	8 45	0 0	27 31
52	10 7	12 51	9 1	30♍ 0	27 22
53	10 31	13 19	9 17	30 0	27 13
54	10 57	13 47	9 34	0♎ 0	27 3
55	11 25	14 17	9 51	0 0	26 53
56	11 54	14 47	10 9	30♍ 0	26 43
57	12 25	15 19	10 26	0♎ 0	26 32
58	12 59	15 52	10 45	30♍ 0	26 21
59	13 35	16 26	11 3	0♎ 0	26 9
60	14♋14	17♌ 1	11♍23	30♍ 0	25♎57

4h 4m 0s — 61° 0' 0" — 3 ♊ 3

LAT.	11	12	ASC	2	3
0	0♋55	28♋52	28♌52	1♎ 5	3♏13
5	1 35	0♌ 3	29 56	1 4	2 50
10	2 15	1 13	0♍57	1 2	2 27
15	2 57	2 23	1 56	1 1	2 4
20	3 41	3 35	2 54	0 59	1 41
21	3 50	3 50	3 5	0 59	1 36
22	4 0	4 5	3 17	0 59	1 31
23	4 9	4 20	3 28	0 58	1 26
24	4 19	4 35	3 40	0 58	1 21
25	4 28	4 50	3 52	0 58	1 16
26	4 38	5 5	4 3	0 57	1 11
27	4 48	5 21	4 15	0 57	1 5
28	4 59	5 37	4 27	0 57	1 0
29	5 9	5 53	4 39	0 56	0 55
30	5 20	6 9	4 50	0 56	0 49
31	5 31	6 25	5 2	0 56	0 44
32	5 42	6 42	5 14	0 55	0 38
33	5 53	6 59	5 26	0 55	0 33
34	6 5	7 16	5 38	0 55	0 27
35	6 17	7 34	5 51	0 54	0 21
36	6 30	7 52	6 3	0 54	0 15
37	6 42	8 10	6 15	0 54	0 9
38	6 56	8 28	6 28	0 53	0 3
39	7 9	8 47	6 41	0 53	29♎56
40	7 23	9 6	6 54	0 53	29 50
41	7 37	9 26	7 7	0 52	29 43
42	7 52	9 46	7 20	0 52	29 36
43	8 8	10 6	7 33	0 52	29 29
44	8 24	10 27	7 47	0 51	29 22
45	8 41	10 49	8 0	0 51	29 15
46	8 58	11 11	8 14	0 50	29 7
47	9 16	11 34	8 28	0 50	28 59
48	9 35	11 57	8 43	0 50	28 51
49	9 55	12 21	8 57	0 49	28 43
50	10 15	12 46	9 12	0 49	28 34
51	10 37	13 11	9 27	0 48	28 25
52	11 0	13 38	9 43	0 48	28 16
53	11 24	14 5	9 59	0 47	28 7
54	11 50	14 33	10 15	0 47	27 57
55	12 17	15 2	10 31	0 46	27 46
56	12 46	15 32	10 48	0 46	27 36
57	13 17	16 3	11 5	0 45	27 25
58	13 50	16 35	11 23	0 45	27 13
59	14 26	17 9	11 41	0 44	27 1
60	15♋ 5	17♌44	12♍ 0	0♎44	26♎48

4h 8m 0s — 62° 0' 0" — 4 ♊ 0

LAT.	11	12	ASC	2	3
0	1♋50	29♋49	29♌54	2♎11	4♏16
5	2 30	0♌59	0♍56	2 8	3 52
10	3 10	2 9	1 56	2 4	3 28
15	3 52	3 19	2 53	2 1	3 5
20	4 36	4 30	3 49	1 58	2 40
21	4 45	4 45	4 0	1 58	2 35
22	4 55	4 59	4 12	1 57	2 30
23	5 4	5 14	4 23	1 56	2 25
24	5 14	5 29	4 34	1 56	2 20
25	5 23	5 44	4 45	1 55	2 15
26	5 33	5 59	4 56	1 55	2 10
27	5 43	6 15	5 8	1 54	2 4
28	5 53	6 30	5 19	1 53	1 59
29	6 4	6 46	5 31	1 53	1 53
30	6 15	7 2	5 42	1 52	1 48
31	6 25	7 18	5 54	1 51	1 42
32	6 37	7 35	6 5	1 51	1 36
33	6 48	7 51	6 17	1 50	1 31
34	7 0	8 8	6 28	1 49	1 25
35	7 12	8 26	6 40	1 49	1 19
36	7 24	8 43	6 52	1 48	1 12
37	7 37	9 1	7 4	1 47	1 6
38	7 50	9 19	7 16	1 47	1 0
39	8 3	9 38	7 29	1 46	0 53
40	8 17	9 57	7 41	1 45	0 47
41	8 32	10 16	7 54	1 45	0 40
42	8 46	10 36	8 6	1 44	0 33
43	9 2	10 56	8 19	1 43	0 25
44	9 18	11 17	8 32	1 42	0 18
45	9 34	11 38	8 46	1 41	0 10
46	9 52	12 0	8 59	1 41	0 3
47	10 10	12 22	9 13	1 40	29♎54
48	10 28	12 45	9 27	1 39	29 46
49	10 48	13 9	9 41	1 38	29 38
50	11 9	13 33	9 55	1 37	29 29
51	11 30	13 58	10 10	1 36	29 20
52	11 53	14 24	10 25	1 35	29 10
53	12 17	14 51	10 40	1 35	29 0
54	12 42	15 18	10 56	1 34	28 50
55	13 9	15 47	11 11	1 33	28 39
56	13 38	16 16	11 28	1 32	28 28
57	14 9	16 47	11 44	1 31	28 17
58	14 42	17 19	12 1	1 29	28 5
59	15 17	17 52	12 19	1 28	27 52
60	15♋56	18♌26	12♍37	1♎27	27♎39

4h 12m 0s — 63° 0' 0" — 4 ♊ 57

LAT.	11	12	ASC	2	3
0	2♋45	0♌47	0♍57	3♎16	5♏18
5	3 25	1 57	1 57	3 11	4 53
10	4 5	3 5	2 55	3 7	4 29
15	4 47	4 14	3 50	3 2	4 5
20	5 31	5 25	4 45	2 57	3 40
21	5 40	5 39	4 55	2 57	3 35
22	5 49	5 54	5 6	2 56	3 30
23	5 59	6 8	5 17	2 55	3 24
24	6 8	6 23	5 28	2 54	3 19
25	6 18	6 38	5 39	2 53	3 14
26	6 28	6 53	5 50	2 52	3 8
27	6 38	7 8	6 1	2 51	3 3
28	6 48	7 24	6 12	2 50	2 57
29	6 58	7 39	6 23	2 49	2 52
30	7 9	7 55	6 34	2 48	2 46
31	7 20	8 11	6 45	2 47	2 40
32	7 31	8 27	6 56	2 46	2 34
33	7 43	8 44	7 7	2 45	2 28
34	7 54	9 1	7 19	2 44	2 22
35	8 6	9 18	7 30	2 43	2 16
36	8 18	9 35	7 42	2 42	2 10
37	8 31	9 53	7 53	2 41	2 3
38	8 44	10 11	8 5	2 40	1 57
39	8 58	10 29	8 17	2 39	1 50
40	9 11	10 48	8 29	2 38	1 43
41	9 26	11 7	8 41	2 37	1 36
42	9 40	11 26	8 53	2 36	1 29
43	9 56	11 46	9 6	2 35	1 21
44	10 12	12 7	9 18	2 33	1 14
45	10 28	12 27	9 31	2 32	1 6
46	10 45	12 49	9 44	2 31	0 58
47	11 3	13 11	9 57	2 30	0 50
48	11 22	13 33	10 11	2 29	0 41
49	11 41	13 57	10 24	2 27	0 32
50	12 2	14 21	10 38	2 26	0 23
51	12 23	14 45	10 52	2 25	0 14
52	12 46	15 11	11 7	2 23	0 4
53	13 10	15 37	11 21	2 22	29♎54
54	13 35	16 4	11 36	2 20	29 43
55	14 2	16 32	11 52	2 19	29 32
56	14 30	17 1	12 7	2 17	29 21
57	15 0	17 31	12 23	2 16	29 9
58	15 33	18 2	12 40	2 14	28 56
59	16 8	18 34	12 57	2 12	28 44
60	16♋46	19♌ 8	13♍14	2♎11	28♎30

FEBRUARY 1954

LONGITUDE

Day	Sid. Time	☉	☽	☽ 12 Hour	Mean ☊	True ☊	☿	♀	♂	♃	♄	♅	♆	♇
	h m s	° ' "	° ' "	° ' "	° '	° '	° '	° '	° '	° '	° '	° '	° '	° '
1	8 42 40	11♒ 35 43	7♑ 27 41	14♑ 10 25	23♑ 6	23♑ 59	23♒ 37	12♒ 4	25♏ 2	16♊ 34R	9♏ 7	20♋ 13R	26♎ 3R	24♌ 5R
2	8 46 36	12 36 37	20 59 0	27 53 18	23 3	24 0R	25 20	13 20	25 36	16 32	9 9	20 10	26 3	24 4
3	8 50 33	13 37 31	4♒ 53 2	11♒ 57 47	23 0	23 59	27 3	14 35	26 11	16 30	9 11	20 8	26 3	24 2
4	8 54 29	14 38 23	19 7 0	26 20 3	22 57	23 58	28 45	15 50	26 44	16 29	9 12	20 6	26 3	24 1
5	8 58 26	15 39 15	3♓ 36 9	10♓ 54 30	22 54	23 56	0♓ 25	17 6	27 18	16 28	9 13	20 3	26 3	24 0
6	9 2 23	16 40 4	18 14 12	25 34 23	22 50	23 53	2 3	18 21	27 52	16 27	9 15	20 1	26 2	23 58
7	9 6 19	17 40 53	2♈ 54 12	10♈ 12 51	22 47	23 49	3 38	19 36	28 26	16 26	9 16	19 59	26 2	23 57
8	9 10 16	18 41 40	17 29 36	24 43 50	22 44	23 46	5 11	20 52	29 0	16 25	9 17	19 57	26 2	23 55
9	9 14 12	19 42 26	1♉ 55 2	9♉ 2 47	22 41	23 44	6 41	22 7	29 33	16 25	9 18	19 55	26 1	23 54
10	9 18 9	20 43 10	16 6 49	23 6 57	22 38	23 43D	8 6	23 22	0♐ 7	16 25D	9 18	19 52	26 1	23 52
11	9 22 5	21 43 52	0♊ 3 6	6♊ 55 14	22 35	23 43	9 27	24 37	0 40	16 25	9 19	19 50	26 0	23 51
12	9 26 2	22 44 33	13 43 26	20 27 46	22 31	23 44	10 42	25 52	1 13	16 25	9 20	19 48	26 0	23 49
13	9 29 58	23 45 12	27 8 24	3♋ 45 27	22 28	23 46	11 51	27 8	1 46	16 25	9 20	19 46	25 59	23 48
14	9 33 55	24 45 49	10♋ 19 5	16 49 28	22 25	23 47R	12 53	28 23	2 20	16 26	9 21	19 44	25 59	23 46
15	9 37 52	25 46 25	23 16 43	29 40 59	22 22	23 48	13 48	29 38	2 53	16 27	9 21	19 42	25 58	23 45
16	9 41 48	26 47 0	6♌ 2 23	12♌ 21 1	22 19	23 47	14 34	0♓ 53	3 25	16 28	9 21	19 40	25 57	23 43
17	9 45 45	27 47 32	18 36 59	24 50 23	22 16	23 44	15 12	2 8	3 58	16 29	9 21R	19 38	25 57	23 42
18	9 49 41	28 48 3	1♍ 1 17	7♍ 9 48	22 12	23 40	15 40	3 23	4 31	16 31	9 21	19 37	25 56	23 40
19	9 53 38	29 48 32	13 16 4	19 20 10	22 9	23 34	15 59	4 38	5 4	16 32	9 21	19 35	25 55	23 39
20	9 57 34	0♓ 49 0	25 22 19	1♎ 22 40	22 6	23 27	16 7R	5 54	5 36	16 34	9 21	19 33	25 55	23 37
21	10 1 31	1 49 27	7♎ 21 29	13 19 1	22 3	23 20	16 5	7 9	6 9	16 36	9 20	19 31	25 54	23 36
22	10 5 27	2 49 51	19 15 35	25 11 33	22 0	23 13	15 53	8 24	6 41	16 38	9 20	19 29	25 53	23 35
23	10 9 24	3 50 15	1♏ 7 19	7♏ 3 20	21 56	23 7	15 32	9 39	7 13	16 41	9 19	19 28	25 52	23 33
24	10 13 21	4 50 37	13 0 6	18 58 8	21 53	23 3	15 1	10 54	7 45	16 43	9 19	19 26	25 51	23 32
25	10 17 17	5 50 58	24 58 0	1♐ 0 18	21 50	23 0	14 21	12 9	8 17	16 46	9 18	19 25	25 50	23 30
26	10 21 14	6 51 17	7♐ 5 37	13 14 35	21 47	23 0D	13 34	13 24	8 49	16 49	9 17	19 23	25 50	23 29
27	10 25 10	7 51 35	19 27 49	25 45 55	21 44	23 0	12 41	14 39	9 21	16 52	9 16	19 22	25 49	23 27
28	10 29 7	8♓ 51 52	2♑ 9 26	8♑ 38 54	21♑ 41	23♑ 1	11♓ 44	15♓ 54	9♐ 52	16♊ 56	9♏ 15	19♋ 20	25♎ 48	23♌ 26

DECLINATION and LATITUDE

Day	☉ Decl	☽ Decl	☽ Lat	☽ 12 Hr. Decl	☿ Decl	☿ Lat	♀ Decl	♀ Lat	♂ Decl	♂ Lat	♃ Decl	♃ Lat	♄ Decl	♄ Lat
1	17S19	24S44	1S30	23S35	15S 4	1S30	18S20	1S12	18S 4	0N59	22N24	0S22	12S12	2N28
2	17 2	22 5	0 17	20 14	14 22	1 23	17 60	1 13	18 13	0 59	22 24	0 22	12 12	2 29
3	16 44	18 5	0N60	15 39	13 40	1 15	17 39	1 15	18 21	0 58	22 24	0 22	12 12	2 29
4	16 27	12 58	2 14	10 6	12 57	1 7	17 18	1 16	18 30	0 58	22 24	0 22	12 12	2 29
5	16 9	7 4	3 21	3 56	12 13	0 57	16 56	1 17	18 38	0 57	22 24	0 21	12 13	2 29
6	15 51	0 44	4 15	2N28	11 29	0 47	16 34	1 18	18 46	0 57	22 24	0 21	12 13	2 30
7	15 32	5N38	4 53	8 43	10 45	0 37	16 12	1 19	18 54	0 56	22 24	0 21	12 13	2 30
8	15 14	11 40	5 12	14 26	10 0	0 25	15 49	1 20	19 2	0 56	22 24	0 21	12 13	2 30
9	14 55	16 60	5 11	19 17	9 16	0 13	15 25	1 21	19 9	0 55	22 25	0 21	12 13	2 30
10	14 35	21 17	4 50	22 58	8 32	0N 0	15 1	1 22	19 17	0 55	22 25	0 20	12 13	2 31
11	14 16	24 17	4 13	25 14	7 49	0 14	14 37	1 22	19 25	0 54	22 25	0 20	12 13	2 31
12	13 56	25 48	3 22	25 58	7 7	0 28	14 12	1 23	19 32	0 54	22 25	0 20	12 13	2 31
13	13 36	25 46	2 21	25 11	6 28	0 43	13 47	1 24	19 39	0 53	22 25	0 20	12 13	2 31
14	13 16	24 16	1 13	23 1	5 50	0 58	13 22	1 24	19 46	0 52	22 26	0 20	12 13	2 32
15	12 56	21 29	0 3	19 42	5 14	1 14	12 56	1 25	19 53	0 52	22 26	0 19	12 13	2 32
16	12 35	17 42	1S 6	15 30	4 42	1 29	12 30	1 25	20 0	0 51	22 26	0 19	12 12	2 32
17	12 15	13 10	2 11	10 43	4 13	1 45	12 3	1 26	20 7	0 51	22 27	0 19	12 12	2 32
18	11 54	8 10	3 9	5 34	3 48	2 1	11 36	1 26	20 14	0 50	22 27	0 19	12 12	2 33
19	11 33	2 56	3 57	0 17	3 26	2 16	11 9	1 26	20 20	0 49	22 27	0 19	12 12	2 33
20	11 11	2S21	4 33	4S56	3 9	2 31	10 42	1 27	20 27	0 49	22 28	0 19	12 11	2 33
21	10 50	7 28	4 58	9 56	2 57	2 45	10 14	1 27	20 33	0 48	22 28	0 18	12 11	2 33
22	10 28	12 18	5 9	14 32	2 50	2 58	9 46	1 27	20 39	0 47	22 28	0 18	12 11	2 34
23	10 6	16 39	5 6	18 36	2 47	3 10	9 18	1 27	20 45	0 47	22 29	0 18	12 10	2 34
24	9 44	20 22	4 51	21 56	2 50	3 20	8 49	1 27	20 51	0 46	22 29	0 18	12 10	2 34
25	9 22	23 16	4 23	24 21	2 57	3 29	8 21	1 27	20 57	0 45	22 30	0 18	12 9	2 34
26	8 60	25 9	3 43	25 40	3 9	3 35	7 52	1 27	21 3	0 44	22 30	0 17	12 9	2 34
27	8 37	25 52	2 51	25 45	3 25	3 40	7 22	1 26	21 8	0 44	22 31	0 17	12 8	2 35
28	8S15	25S16	1S50	24S27	3S44	3N42	6S53	1S26	21S14	0N43	22N31	0S17	12S 8	2N35

Day	♅ Decl	♅ Lat	♆ Decl	♆ Lat	♇ Decl	♇ Lat
1	22N25	0N30	8S28	1N43	22N58	10N 4
5	22 26	0 30	8 28	1 43	23 0	10 5
9	22 27	0 30	8 27	1 43	23 3	10 5
13	22 29	0 30	8 26	1 43	23 5	10 5
17	22 30	0 30	8 25	1 44	23 7	10 6
21	22 31	0 30	8 24	1 44	23 10	10 6
25	22N32	0N30	8S22	1N44	23N12	10N 6

☽ PHENOMENA

d	h	m	
3	15	56	●
10	8	30	☽
17	19	18	○
25	23	29	☾

d	h	° '
6	3	0
12	11	25N58
19	13	0
27	1	25S53
2	5	0
8	10	5N14
15	1	0
22	8	5S 9

VOID OF COURSE ☽

Last Aspect		☽ Ingress		
2	8am50	2	♒	3pm38
4	6pm 4	4	♓	6pm 4
6	4pm23	6	♈	7pm15
8	2pm 9	8	♉	8pm47
10	1pm40	10	♊	11pm55
12	11pm59	13	♋	5am10
15	5am 1	15	♌	12pm36
17	7pm18	17	♍	10pm 1
19	12pm27	20	♎	9am15
22	1pm23	22	♏	9pm44
24	9pm 5	25	♐	10am 1
27	12pm 4	27	♑	7pm58

d	h	
6	6	PERIGEE
22	7	APOGEE

DAILY ASPECTARIAN

Day	Aspect	Time
1	☽∠☿	2am23
M	☽⚼♇	2 55
	☽✱♄	2 59
	☽∠♂	4 50
	☿☍♇	6 29
	☉⚺☽	8 1
	☽⚺♀	9 7
	♀∥♂	1pm11
	☽⚻♃	4 12
	☽#♇	5 13
	☽#♅	9 32
	☽#♃	9 40
	☽☍♅	10 35
2	☽⚻♇	5am22
T	☿□♂	5 35
	☽✱♂	8 24
	☽⚺☿	8 40
	☽□♆	8 50
	☿△♆	9 58
	☽⚼♃	6pm14
	♂⚺♆	6 48
	☽∥♂	10 37
3	☽∥♀	2am24
W	☉∥☽	7 12
	☽□♄	7 18
	☉☌☽	3pm56
	☽☌♀	5 59
	☽△♃	7 36
4	☽∥☿	0am 5
Th	☽⚻♅	1 38
	☽∥♄	3 16
	☽☍♇	8 9
	☽△♆	11 31
	♀△♃	12pm 6
	☽□♂	1 11
	☿ ♓	6 4
	☽☌☿	6 4
	☽∥♆	6 32
5	☿∥♄	0am27
F	☽⚼♅	2 23
	☽△♄	9 15
	☽⚼♆	12pm13
	☉△♃	6 49
	☽□♃	9 4
	☉⚺☽	9 15
6	☽⚺♀	0am12
S	☽△♅	2 55
	☽⚻♇	9 22
	☽⚼♄	9 50
	☽⚻♆	12pm45
	☽△♂	4 23
	☉∠☽	11 37
7	☽⚺☿	1am21
Su	☽∠♀	3 3
	♀⚻♅	7 1
	☽⚼♇	9 54
	☽⚻♄	10 27
	☽#♆	10 57
	☽#☿	3pm54
	☽⚼♂	5 59
	☿⚼♅	8 18
	☽✱♃	10 14
8	☉✱☽	2am 8
M	☽#♄	2 18
	☽□♅	4 3
	☽∠☿	4 59
	☽✱♀	6 6
	☽△♇	10 38
	☽☍♆	2pm 9
	☉#☽	2 41
	☽#♀	5 0
	☽⚻♂	7 53
	☽∠♃	11 10
9	☉⚻♅	4am37
T	☽✱☿	8 54
	☽#♂	11 37
	☽☍♄	12pm26
	♂ ♐	7 18
10	☽⚺♃	0am31
W	☿∥♆	2 55
	☽✱♅	6 25
	☽∥♃	7 47
	☽∥♅	8 9
	☉□☽	8 30
	♀☍♇	9 27
	♃SD	9 32
	☽∥♇	12pm48
	☽□♇	1 17
	☽□♀	1 40
	☽⚻♆	4 59
	☿△♄	9 41
11	☽☍♂	1am 7
Th	☽∠♅	8 20
	☽⚻♄	4pm14
	☽□☿	6 7
	☽⚼♆	7 11
12	♀△♆	2am19
F	☽☌♃	4 47
	☿⚼♆	5 58
	☽⚺♅	10 48
	☉△☽	5pm24
	☽✱♇	5 59
	☽⚼♄	6 57
	☽△♆	9 55
	☽△♀	11 59
13	☉☍♇	1am 0
S	☽⚻♂	8 45
	☽∠♇	9pm10
	☽△♄	10 13
	☉⚼☽	10 54
14	☽△☿	5am 6
Su	☽⚼♀	6 14
	☽∥♇	11 16
	☽⚺♃	11 17
	☽⚼♂	1pm30
	☽∥♅	4 24
	☽∥♃	4 50
	☽☌♅	5 21
	☉∥♀	11 23
15	☽⚺♇	0am52
M	☉△♆	4 34
	☽□♆	5 1
	☉⚻☽	5 4
	♀ ♓	7 2
	☽#♂	10 28
	☽⚼☿	11 3
	☽⚻♀	1pm12
	☽∠♃	3 21
	☽△♂	6 50
16	☽□♄	6am17
T	♀∥♄	3pm39
	☽⚻☿	5 8
	☽✱♃	7 54
17	☽⚺♅	1am58
W	☉∥♄	2 42
	☽#♄	4 47
	☉#☽	4 56
	☽#♀	6 5
	♄SR	6 18
	☽☌♇	9 46
	☽✱♆	2pm 8
	☉☍☽	7 18
	☽#♆	10 53
18	♂⚼♅	3am50
Th	☽☍♀	5 9
	☽∠♅	6 59
	☽□♂	7 8
	☽✱♄	4pm18
	☽∠♆	7 23
	☽#☿	9 33
	♀⚼♅	10 49
19	☉ ♓	4am33
F	☽☍☿	5 27
	☽□♃	6 28
	☽✱♅	12pm27
	♀□♂	2 12
	☽⚺♇	8 32
	☽∠♄	9 57
20	☽⚺♆	1am 4
S	☽∥☿	3 34
	☿SR	7 38
	☉⚻☽	11 53
	☽✱♂	9pm27
	☽⚻♀	11 31
21	☽∠♇	2am30
Su	☽⚺♄	3 59
	☽∥♆	4 26
	☽∥♀	12pm18
	☉∥☽	3 19
	☽⚻☿	5 20
	☽△♃	6 41
	☉⚼☽	8 51
	☽∥♄	11 24
22	☽□♅	0am28
M	☽∠♂	5 8
	☽✱♇	8 43
	☽⚼♀	9 21
	☽☌♆	1pm23
	♀△♄	5 53
	☽⚼☿	10 50
23	☽⚼♃	1am 8
T	☉△☽	6 0
	☽⚺♂	12pm55
	☉⚼♅	2 32
	☽☌♄	4 34
	☽△♀	7 15
	♀⚼♆	11 14
24	☽∥♂	3am44
W	☽△☿	3 51
	☽⚻♃	7 31
	☽△♅	12pm55
	☽#♃	4 50
	☽#♅	5 8
	☽□♇	9 5
	♀∥♆	10 34
	☽#♇	11 21
25	☽⚺♆	1am44
Th	☽⚼♅	6pm41
	☉□☽	11 29
26	☿☌♀	2am 2
F	☽☌♂	3 32
	☽⚺♄	4 17
	☽∠♆	7 17
	☽□☿	11 49
	☽□♀	1pm41
	☽☍♃	7 0
	♂⚺♄	8 38
	☽⚻♅	11 48
27	☽△♇	7am36
S	☽∠♄	9 9
	☽✱♆	12pm 4
	☉∥♆	5 21
28	☉△♄	9am 8
Su	☽⚼♇	11 35
	☽✱♄	1pm 5
	☉✱☽	1 25
	☽⚺♂	2 50
	☽✱☿	4 22
	♀□♃	8 47
	☿⚼♆	10 23

Calculation Form

1. Name: **Patricia Hearst**

   Source of Data: **Contemporary Sidereal**

2. Birthdate: **February 20, 1954**

3. Birthplace: **Berkeley, California**

   Longitude: **122W16**　　Latitude: **37N52**

4. Birthtime (use 24-hour system):

Daylight Saving Time (if applicable)	___h ___m ___s
Pacific Standard Time	**18**h **01**m **00**s
+ *or* − hours from birthplace to Greenwich	**+8**h ___m ___s
Greenwich Birthtime	**26**h **01**m **00**s
−24 if Greenwich Birthtime is over 24 hours	**2**h **01**m **00**s
Altered Birthdate if Greenwich Birthtime is over 24 hours	**Feb. 21, 1954**

5. Local Sidereal Time:

Sidereal Time	**10**h **01**m **31**s
+ Greenwich Birthtime	**2**h **01**m **00**s
+9.86 seconds × Greenwich Birthtime	___h ___m **20**s
= Greenwich Sidereal Time of Birth	**12**h **02**m **51**s
+ or − Longitude Time Equivalent (E+, W−)	**8**h **09**m **04**s
= Local Sidereal Time of Birth	**3**h **53**m **47**s

Sidereal Time comes from the ephemeris for the altered birthdate. Greenwich Birthtime comes from 4. above. The multiplication of the Greenwich Birthtime by 9.86 seconds and the addition of the resultant figure to the Greenwich Birthtime converts the clock time to sidereal time. The formula for the hand calculator is: [(minutes of Greenwich Birthtime ÷ 60) + hours of Greenwich Birthtime] × 9.86 seconds. The result is in seconds of time. For Patricia Hearst the Greenwich Birthtime is 2 hours and 1 minute. 1 ÷ 60 = .0167. .0167 + 2 = 2.0167. 2.0167 × 9.86 = 19.8843, so the adjustment, rounded off, to be added to the Greenwich Birthtime is 20 seconds.

To convert longitude into time, 15 degrees of longitude = 1 hour of time; 1 degree of longitude = 4 minutes of time; 1 minute of longitude = 4 seconds of time. Patricia Hearst was born in Berkeley, California: longitude 122w16. 122 ÷ 15 = 8 hours with 2 degrees left over. 2 degrees × 4 minutes = 8 minutes. 16 minutes of longitude × 4 seconds = 64 seconds. The Longitude Time Equivalent, therefore, is 8 hours, 8 minutes and 64 seconds or 8 hours, 9 minutes and 4 seconds.

Since Berkeley, California, is west of Greenwich, the Longitude Time Equivalent is subtracted from the Greenwich Sidereal Time. If Berkeley were east of Greenwich, the Longitude Time Equivalent would be added to the Greenwich Sidereal Time.

When subtracting the Longitude Time Equivalent from the Greenwich Sidereal Time, if the seconds of the Longitude Time Equivalent are greater than the seconds of the Greenwich Sidereal Time, 1 minute must be subtracted from the minutes column of the Greenwich Sidereal Time and added to the seconds column as 60 seconds. If, as is true in this case, the minutes of the Longitude Time Equivalent are greater than the minutes of the Greenwich Sidereal Time, 1 hour must be subtracted from the hours column of the Greenwich Sidereal Time and added to the minutes column as 60 minutes. If the hours of the Longitude Time Equivalent are greater than the hours of the Greenwich Sidereal Time, 24 hours must be added to the hours column of the Greenwich Sidereal Time. (24 hours are just added, without being subtracted from anywhere.) The answer is the local Sidereal Time of Birth.

House Cusps. Two interpolations must be made for houses 11, 12, 1 (Asc.), 2, 3—one for Local Sidereal Time and one for latitude. For the 10th house (MC) only one interpolation must be made, for Local Sidereal Time, because the 10th house is the point due south on the ecliptic (overhead) thus no latitude is involved.

To determine the Sidereal Time Factor turn to the Tables of Houses in the ephemeris, and find the Sidereal Times between which the Local Sidereal Time of Birth falls. The Sidereal Times are given in the upper left-hand corner of each block. They are given in hours, minutes and seconds and are in 4 minute (240 second) intervals. Subtract the smaller Sidereal Time from the Local Sidereal Time. Divide by 240. For Patricia Hearst, Local Sidereal Time of Birth is 3 hours, 53 minutes, 47 seconds. In the Tables of Houses, this time falls between 3 hours, 52 minutes, 00 seconds and 3 hours, 56 minutes, 00 seconds. 3h 53m 47s − 3h 52m 00s = 1m 47s, or 107 seconds. 107 ÷ 240 = .4458, which is Patricia Hearst's Sidereal Time Factor.

To determine the Latitude Factor note the latitude of the birthplace. Divide the minutes of latitude by 60. For Patricia Hearst, latitude of birth is 37N 52. 52÷60 = .8667, which is Patricia Hearst's Latitude Factor. Record Sidereal Time Factor and Latitude Factor under 6 on the Calculation Form. All interpolations for Patricia Hearst will be between the Sidereal Times of 3h 52m 00s and 3h 56m 00s and the latitudes of 37° and 38°.

Interpolating

10th House (MC): Find the distance the MC traveled from the earlier Sidereal Time to the later Sidereal Time. The middle of the top section of each block in the Table of Houses lists the position of the MC. Subtract the earlier MC from the later MC to get the distance (a). (There's no latitude given since the MC is the same for all latitudes). Multiply the distance (converted into minutes if over 1 degree) by the Sidereal Time Factor and add the result to the earlier MC. The Sidereal Time Factor may be placed in the memory of the calculator. The formula would be Distance × Memory Recall = minutes MC traveled to Local Sidereal Time of Birth (b).

For Patricia Hearst:

10th House Cusp (MC):

MC for later Sidereal Time		♊ 1° 08'
MC for earlier Sidereal Time		♊ 0° 11'
(Subtract)	(a)	0° 57'
STF × (a)	= (b)	25.4125'
Earlier MC		♊ 0° 11'
+ (b)	= MC	♊ 0° 36'

57'' × the Sidereal Time Factor or Memory Recall, .4458, = 25.4125. Record next to STF × (a). Earlier MC, 0° 11', + (b), 25.4125', = MC, 0°♊36' rounded off.

If the MC for the earlier Sidereal Time were 29° ♉ 13' and the MC for the later Sidereal Time were 0° ♊ 11', a sign or 30° would have to be added to the later MC, so that the subtraction could be done.

As stated previously, there are two interpolations for the 11th, 12th, 1st (Asc.), 2nd and 3rd houses. The procedure for obtaining the Sidereal correction for these houses is the same as for the 10th house. But now we take latitude into consideration.

We use the house cusps given for the lower whole degree latitude. (For Patricia Hearst, 37° latitude under 3h 52m 00s and 3h 56m 00s Sidereal Times).

Now write the 11th house cusp given for the later Sidereal Time for the lower whole degree of latitude, and write the 11th house cusp given for the earlier Sidereal Time for the lower whole degree of latitude. Subtract and get (c); multiply by STF or Memory Recall and get (d). Follow the same procedure for the 12th, 1st (Asc.), 2nd and 3rd houses.

For Patricia Hearst:

11th House Cusp:

11th for later Sidereal Time	♋ 4°54′
11th for earlier Sidereal Time	♋ 3°59′
(Subtract) (c)	0°55′
STF × (c) = (d)	24.5190′

The lower whole degree of latitude is 37°. The 11th cusp for 37° under the Sidereal Time of 3h 52m 00s is 3° ♋ 59′. The 11th cusp for 37° under the Sidereal Time of 3h 56m 00s is 4° ♋ 54′.

To obtain your Latitude Factor, use the house cusp positions that are given for the two latitudes between which the birth locality latitude falls. Use the positions of the house cusps under the earlier Sidereal Time. By Sidereal Time the house cusps always move forward; by latitude the cusps may move forward or backward. If the house cusp for the later latitude is greater than the house cusp for the earlier latitude, the house cusp is moving forward; if smaller, it is moving backward. Of course 0° of a later sign is larger than 29° of an earlier sign.

Clear the Sidereal Time Factor from the memory, and replace it with the Latitude Factor. Under 11th House Cusp enter the larger house cusp of the two latitudes for the earlier Sidereal Time. Enter the smaller house cusp of the two latitudes for the earlier Sidereal Time. Subtract and get (e); multiply by memory (Latitude Factor). The result is (f) which equals the distance the house cusp moved to birth locality latitude. Write the result in the space after LF × (e) =.

If the house cusp has become larger by latitude, circle +; if it has become smaller, circle −. Add (f) to the house cusp obtained with the sidereal correction if the house cusp has moved forward by latitude; subtract (f) if the house cusp has moved backward by latitude. The result will be the accurate 11th house cusp.

Patricia Hearst's birth latitude is between 37° and 38°. Under 37° for the 11th house we find 3° ♋ 59'. Under 38° for the 11th house we find 4° ♋ 12'. The house cusp is moving forward by latitude, so we circle that + next to (f). We subtract 3°59' from 4°12'. The difference is 13 minutes. 13' × LF, which is .8667 = 11.2667. We add this number to the house cusp with the sidereal correction, and the result is the accurate 11th house cusp.

Larger house cusp		♋ 4 ° 12 '
Smaller house cusp		♋ 3 ° 59 '
(Subtract)	= (e)	° 13 '
LF × (e)	= (f)	11.2667 '
Earlier 11th house cusp		♋ 3 ° 59 '
+ (d)	= ♋	3 ° 83.52 '
+ or − (f) =11th house cusp	♋	3 ° 95
	= ♋	4° 35'

Follow the same procedure for the other house cusps.

Planets and Points. Planetary positions are given for each day for midnight at Greenwich. One must first determine how much a planet moved from the Greenwich Birthdate to the day after Greenwich Birthdate. The distance is multiplied by the Constant (Greenwich Birthtime ÷ 24), and the result is added to (if the planet is moving forward) or subtracted from (if the planet is moving backward) the position of the planet at 0 hours on the Greenwich Birthdate.

To place the Constant in the memory of the calculator: enter the minutes of the Greenwich Birthtime in the calculator; divide by 60; add the hours of the Greenwich Birthtime, and divide the total by 24. Place the result in the memory, and record the result next to Constant.

Patricia Hearst's Greenwich Birthtime is 2 hours, 1 minute. 1 ÷ 60 + 2 ÷ 24 = .0840.

The Sun always moves forward, and the position is given in degrees, minutes and seconds. Write the position of the Sun (the Sun column is the second column in the ephemeris) for the day after the Greenwich Birthdate next to Position for later date. Write the Sun position for the Greenwich Birthdate next to Position for earlier date. Subtract. The result will be either minutes and seconds or 1 degree, minutes and seconds. Record next to Distance traveled.

If the result of the initial subtraction is 1 degree, minutes and seconds, convert the 1 degree to 60 minutes, add the 60 minutes to the minutes column and proceed. Enter the seconds of Distance traveled in the calculator, divide by 60 and add this figure to the minutes. Multiply by the Constant. The number to the left of the decimal in the calculator is the minutes to be added to the earlier Sun position. Write that number next to (a) in the minutes column. Subtract the minutes from the calculator and multiply the number to the right of the decimal by 60. The number to the left of the decimal will now be seconds. Write this number next to (a) in the seconds column. Add the minutes and seconds to the earlier Sun position. The result will be the position of the Sun at birth.

Patricia Hearst's Greenwich Birthdate is February 21, 1954. We look at February, 1954 in the ephemeris The Sun's position at 0 hours on February 21, 1954 is 1° ♓ 49′ 27″ and at hours on February 22, 1954 is 2° ♓ 49′ 51″

Constant = .0840

☉   (Always moves forward)

Position for later date	♓ 2 °49′51″
Position for earlier date	♓ 1 °49′27″
Distance traveled	1° 0′24″
× Constant = (a)	5′4″
Earlier position	♓ 1°49′27″
+ (a) =Birth position ☉	♓ 1°54′31″

The Moon always moves forward, and the position is given in degrees, minutes and seconds. With the Moon we calculate only the degrees and minutes. If the seconds column is less than 30, use the minutes given in the ephemeris; if 30 or more, add one minute to the minutes column. Subtract the Moon position (column next to the Sun, not "Moon 12 hours") for the Greenwich Birthdate from the Moon position for the day after the Greenwich Birthdate. The answer will be in degrees and minutes. Divide the minutes by 60; add the degrees; multiply by the Constant. The number to the left of the decimal will be the degrees. Write this number next to (b) in the degrees column. Subtract the degrees from the calculator; multiply the remainder by 60. The number to the left of the decimal will be the number of minutes to be added to the earlier Moon position. If the number after the decimal is 5 or more, add 1 minute to the minutes. Write this number next to (b) in the minutes column. Add to the earlier Moon position. The result is the position of the Moon at birth.

☾   (Always moves forward)

Position for later date		♎ 19 ° 16 '
Position for earlier date		♎ 7 ° 21 '
Distance traveled		11 ° 55 '
× Constant	= (b)	1 °
Earlier position		♎ 7 ° 21 '
+ (b)	= Birth position ☾	♎ 8 ° 21 '

The Mean Nodes always move backward; so the position for the later date is always smaller than that for the Greenwich Birthdate. Subtract the later position from the earlier position; multiply the result by the Constant, and subtract the product from the earlier position.

The planets other than the Sun or Moon, may move forward or backward. If the position of the planet for the day *after* the Greenwich Birthdate is smaller than the position for the Greenwich Birthdate, the planet is going backward or is retrograde. The position of the other planets is given in degrees and minutes. Subtract as with the Sun, the Moon and the Nodes; multiply the result by the Constant. Then, add to the Greenwich Birthdate position if the planet is going forward, or subtract from the Greenwich Birthdate position if the planet is going backward.

Mars, Jupiter, Saturn, Uranus, Neptune and Pluto always move a distance of less than a degree. Mercury and Venus usually move more than a degree. If they do move a degree or more, convert the degrees to minutes, and add that number to the minutes before placing them in the calculator. Then multiply by the Constant. The number to the left of the decimal will be the minutes to be added to the earlier position, or subtracted from it if the planet is retrograde.

Since the distance Mars, Jupiter, Saturn, Uranus, Neptune and Pluto travel will always be in minutes (and the distance of Mercury and Venus has already been converted into minutes), there is no division by 60 when the distance is placed in the calculator. Simply enter the number of minutes in the calculator, and multiply by the Constant. As stated above, the number to the left of the decimal will be the number to be added to, or subtracted from, the Greenwich Birthdate position of the planet. If the first number to the right of the decimal is less than 5, record the number of minutes to the left of the decimal; if 5 or more, add 1 minute and record.

For Patricia Hearst, at midnight on February 21, 1954 Venus was at 7° ♓ 09' and at midnight on February 22, at 8° ♓ 24'.

♀ (May move forward or backward)

Larger	♓	8 °	24 '
Smaller	♓	7 °	09 '
Distance traveled		1 °	15 '
× Constant	= (e)		6.3 '
Earlier position	♓	7 °	09 '
+ or − (e) =Birth position	♀ ♓	7 °	15 '

The Part of Fortune is Ascendant + Moon − Sun. Write the number of the sign (Aries,1; Taurus,2; etc.), then the degrees and the minutes. When subtracting the Sun , if the minutes of the Sun are larger, borrow 1 degree from the degrees column, and add 60 minutes to the minutes column before subtracting; if the degrees of the Sun are larger, borrow 1 sign, and add 30 degrees to the degrees column; if the number of the Sun's sign is larger, just add 12 signs (do not subtract from anywhere).

For Patricia Hearst:

⊗ Part of Fortune (enter signs by number,e.g., Aries, 1; Taurus, 2; etc.)

Ascendant	6	4 °	23 '
+ Moon	7	8 °	22 '
=	13	12 °	45 '
− Sun	12	1 °	55 '
= Part of Fortune ⊗	1	10 °	50 '
= ♈		10°	50 '